Sainsbury's
MASTERCLASS

Sainsbury's
MASTERCLASS
STEP-BY-STEP TO CLASSIC DISHES

Produced in association with Family Circle

Foreword

Sainsbury's is proud to present this splendid collection of Masterclass recipes in book form for the first time.

Masterclass has long been a regular cookery feature in *Family Circle* magazine – and continues to be one of the most popular. That's not surprising, because every month readers can learn exactly how masters of the culinary art transform a classic recipe into their very own speciality.

Over the years, top chefs, restaurateurs and food writers worldwide, have been interviewed to discover the tips and tricks of the trade that turn a good recipe into a great one. Each Masterclass recipe has been photographed step-by-step in the *Family Circle* kitchen so you can see every crucial stage. Whether you are a relative novice or a dab hand at cooking you will find you can tackle the 47 great recipes in this book with confidence, and achieve the same high standards as the masters who have so generously shared their wisdom and experience.

Gilly Cubitt

Gilly Cubitt
Family Circle

Special photography for pages 1, 2–3, 6–7, 32–3, 54–5, 76–7, 134–5, and 176–7
by Vernon Morgan; stylist Maria Jacques, home economist Ricky Turner

Published exclusively for J Sainsbury plc,
Stamford House, Stamford Street, London SE1 9LL
by Cathay Books, an imprint of the Octopus Publishing Group
Michelin House, 81 Fulham Road, London SW3 6RB

First published in volume form 1988
Masterclass series © Family Circle magazine (1984–1988)

Copyright in the individual recipes remains with the original owners.

ISBN 0 86178 532 0

Printed in Italy

Note: For all recipes, quantities are given in both metric and imperial measures. Follow either set but not a mixture of both because they are not interchangeable.

Contents

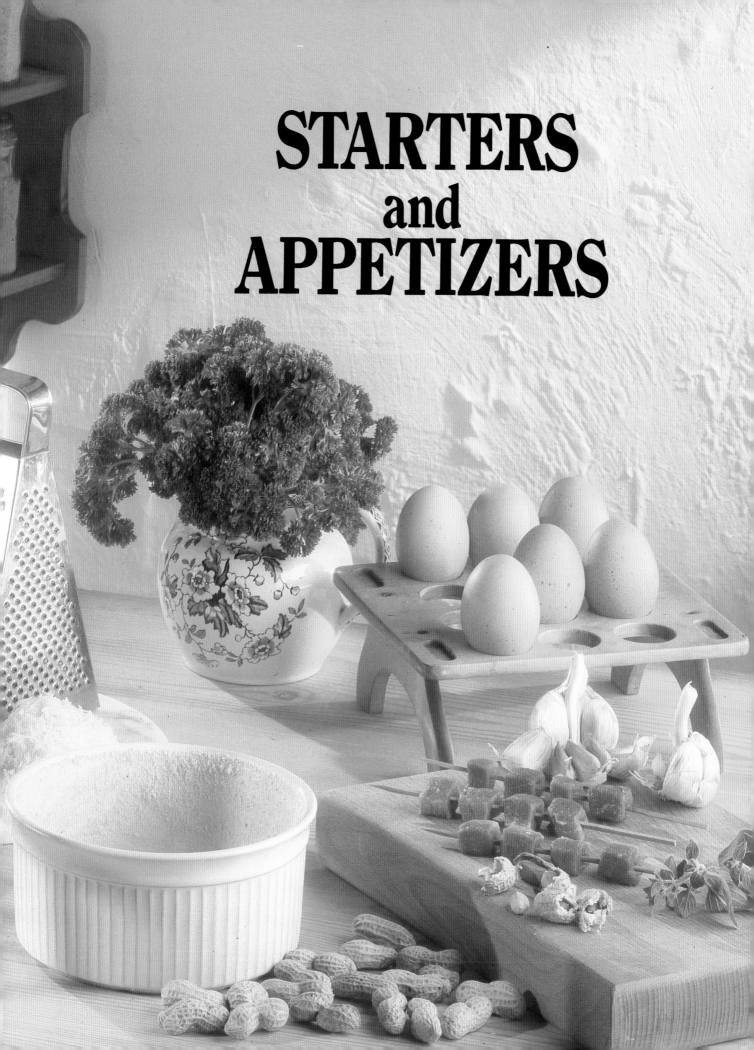

STARTERS
and
APPETIZERS

Susan Campbell's Fish Terrine

Susan Campbell is much more than a recipe writer; she is a fount of knowledge on food and equipment, with a particular enthusiasm for the history of eating. She also illustrates her own books. When collecting recipes on English cookery, she felt that although there were many books on the subject, there was still much more to discover. 'For one thing, I wanted to find out how much of our traditional cooking still survived and how well we were assimilating new influences. Our country produces some of the best raw materials on this earth. Some of our finest products – beef and lamb, game (in particular, venison), lobsters, other shellfish and salmon, both fresh and smoked – are exported at such a pace that we're lucky if we get even a sniff at some of them ourselves.'

Susan is very much an authority on the subject of equipment, having written and illustrated a comprehensive guide to kitchen implements and how to use them. She has a passion for using the right equipment for each preparation or cooking technique. 'It makes life so much easier,' she says. 'You can, of course, rub this fish purée

'Fish terrines are rather in vogue these days. They are just as easy as meat pâtés, more delicate, and extremely pretty, too'

through a round sieve using a wooden spoon, but the wooden spoon is smooth and round and just rotates inside the sieve. It would be much better to use a drum sieve, with tall sides, where you can exert lots of pressure and have something really solid to work on, and one of those old-fashioned, mushroom-shaped mashers, to press the pulp through; a plastic scraper will do almost as well, but a *champignon* is best of all.

'But why sieve the fish purée in the first place? Well, those who don't, obviously don't mind about the quality of the finished product quite so much as I do. The fibres from the fish, bits of skin and gristle get in a tangle in the food processor and have to be removed. But it's so easy when you use the right tools.'

Susan's recipe for fish terrine contains two different mousselines – also called purées – that is to say the lightest of those mousse-type concoctions made with fish, shellfish or meat. Here, one mousseline is white, the other pink, interspersed with bands of fresh green spinach, and the coral and white of scallops. You could take this recipe as a starting point for even more decorative terrines. The white purée could be divided into three: one part stained yellow with saffron, another reddened with tomato purée. You can get speckled effects with chopped watercress or parsley. You could also use thin strips of carrot, string beans or mushrooms to enliven the pattern (blanch firm vegetables before arranging them). Fish terrine is served warm with a cream sauce, flavoured with fish stock or *fumet*.

This kind of recipe may seem a lot of trouble, but make the most of it – go to great lengths to make it really special. Sieve the fish purées, chill all the ingredients and equipment before making the mousselines, use the best cream, make a superb fish *fumet* for the sauce (the perfect accompaniment to this terrine), and then revel in the finished product.

SERVES 8
INGREDIENTS:

1½ lb (750 g) fillets of white fish (sole, whiting, pike or cod)
1 onion
1 carrot
1 leek
1 thin lemon slice
a few stalks of parsley
salt and white pepper
4 egg whites
1 lemon
8 oz (250 g) smoked salmon scraps
8 oz (250 g) fresh spinach leaves
1½ pt (900 ml) double cream
cayenne pepper
butter for greasing terrine
6 scallops (fresh or frozen) or Dublin Bay prawns
TO GARNISH:
spinach leaves, watercress or parsley

Skin 1½ lb (750 g) fish fillets. Place skins, with 1 peeled and thinly sliced onion, carrot and leek, lemon slice, parsley, a pinch of salt, and 1 pt (600 ml) water, in a large saucepan. Bring to boil, remove scum and simmer for 30 min. Chop the fillets into 1 in (2.5 cm) pieces and purée in a food processor.

When the white fish is well chilled, add ¾ pt (450 ml) double cream, a little at a time, beating in each addition vigorously with a wooden spoon. Make sure that the fish absorbs it before adding any more. The mixture should remain very firm. The cream has to be very cold or it will not thicken when added to the fish.

Spread half the pink mousseline over that. Next, prepare the scallop layer. Arrange the corals of 6 scallops in a line down the centre, cut the white parts of the scallops across if they are large and position either side of the corals. Instead of scallops you could use Dublin Bay prawns, chopped into neat pieces.

2

Blend in 2 lightly beaten egg whites. Pass through a sieve to make sure you have a really smooth, fibre-free purée. Grate the rind from a lemon, put in a sieve and pour boiling water over. Drain thoroughly, then add to white fish purée with some salt and white pepper. Cover and refrigerate mixture for about 1 hour.

3

Purée 8oz (250g) smoked salmon scraps in the food processor. Add 2 lightly beaten egg whites and push through sieve. Chill. Rinse 8oz (250g) spinach leaves, and pull away the thick stalks. Blanch for a few seconds in boiling salted water, then plunge in cold water. Drain, then spread out to dry on kitchen paper.

5

For the pink mousseline, beat ¼pt (150ml) double cream into the cold salmon purée, as before. Add 2tbsp lemon juice and a pinch of cayenne pepper. Make sure that the mousseline remains very firm. Preheat the oven to moderate, Gas mark 5, 375°F, 190°C. Generously butter a 1½pt (900ml) terrine.

6

If the mousseline is too sloppy, leave it in the fridge overnight to stiffen. The two mousselines should be roughly the same consistency: if one mixture is heavier, lighten it with a little extra cream. Spread half the white mousseline on the bottom of the terrine and place half the spinach leaves over it in a thin layer.

8

Cover the scallops with remaining salmon mousseline, spinach and white fish in layers, in that order. Smooth top. Cover and place in a wide shallow roasting tin half-filled with boiling water. Bake in the oven until firm, about 45–50 min. Turn out on to warm dish and garnish with spinach, watercress or parsley.

9

Now make the sauce: strain the fish *fumet* (stock) through a sieve lined with a damp cloth. Then boil over a high heat to reduce by half to ½pt (300ml). Add ½pt (300ml) double cream and continue to reduce, over a lower heat, until it coats the back of a spoon. Add a touch of cayenne pepper, salt and pepper.

Terry Tan's Satay

Terry Tan is a complete master of Singaporean cuisine. His first brush with the wok was at the age of 11, after his father died and the family home in Singapore was turned into a boarding house. Suddenly he was required to cook the daily meals for up to 20 people! In between calculus, geography and Keats, he stoked up the family fires and fried up dishes culled from the mixed heritage of his background. He was born in Singapore (then a British colony), to a Chinese/Indonesian father and a Straits Chinese (Sino Malay) mother.

'I learned my cooking at the very best of schools,' Terry admits, 'one that had no gleaming worktops or sophisticated equipment! My school was our big family kitchen, the hub of Singaporean family activity. I not only had the privilege of learning from my mother – in our extended family, I learned a great deal from aunts and uncles who collectively represented culinary arts from Thailand, Malaysia and even Burma. My mother never wrote anything down because she never went to school, but she had a prodigious memory for hundreds of ways of cooking

'Pronounced sah-tay, these delicious skewers of marinated meat with their peanut gravy are the traditional kebab dish of Singapore'

fish, meat and vegetables, and knew exactly which spices went well with each dish. I just learned from instinct.'

Terry remembers, from his boyhood, how local hawkers slung a pole on their shoulders, on each end of which was hung a basket filled with skewers of raw satay, a large pot of peanut gravy and of course, the charcoal brazier. 'People would hail the hawker as he passed in the street, and families would sit down on the kerb and polish off several dozen sticks of beef or chicken satay.

'It took a while before satay became a home-cooked dish, because few families had the privilege of an open hearth or charcoal brazier. Today, satay has reached the Western world as a much more refined and subtly spiced dish, but it is still uniquely Singaporean.' Satay includes some unusual ingredients but Terry suggests alternatives:

Lemon grass has a sharp smell of lemon sherbet when cut. 'Use a little grated lemon rind if it's unobtainable.' Tamarind paste makes the water slightly acid. 'If you can't get it, use a few drops of lemon juice.' Laos root, also called galingale, looks like a ginger root, and has a very delicate flavour. 'Use it if you can find it.'

Cut 2 lb (1 kg) sirloin into ¾ in (2 cm) cubes, removing all gristle and fat. Lightly beat cubes with a steak mallet or rolling pin to allow the marinade to penetrate.

MAKES 30–40 STICKS
INGREDIENTS:

MEAT AND MARINADE:
2 lb (1 kg) sirloin or rump steak
3 tablespoons ground coriander
2 stalks lemon grass (use 3 in (7 cm) from root end)
1 large onion
1 thumb-sized piece fresh ginger root
2 tablespoons oil
6 fl oz (150 ml) canned coconut milk
1 tablespoon salt
2 tablespoons sugar
2 tablespoons ground cumin
1 tablespoon ground aniseed
1 teaspoon ground turmeric
PEANUT GRAVY:
1 large onion
4 cloves garlic
2 stalks lemon grass
10 candlenuts, or cashew or macadamia nuts
1 thumb-sized piece of Laos root (galingale) (optional)
1 thumb-sized piece fresh ginger root
2 tablespoons (about 100 g) tamarind paste or 1 tablespoon lemon juice
1 tablespoon mild chilli powder
4 tablespoons vegetable oil
3 tablespoons sugar
1 to 2 teaspoons salt
12 oz (375 g) good crunchy peanut butter or ground peanuts
TO SERVE:
cucumber wedges
raw onion
compressed rice cubes (see method)

Put the dry-fried coriander, 2 tbsp ground cumin, 1 tbsp ground aniseed, and 1 tsp ground turmeric into a large bowl. Add the blended marinade mixture, and the cubed beef. Cover and marinate for at least 2 hours, preferably overnight.

Heat 4 tbsp oil in the wok or frying pan until almost smoking. Lightly fry the blended mixture for 5 min. Add the remaining acidulated water, 3 tbsp sugar and 1 tsp salt. Add 12 oz (375 g) ground peanuts or good crunchy peanut butter, and simmer for 5 min. Taste and add a little more salt if necessary.

2 Dry-fry 3 tbsp ground coriander in a wok or non-stick frying pan over a low heat for 5 min. Let the wok heat up first, add the spice and stir it while dry-frying. Don't allow it to burn. Remove wok from heat.

3 Assemble marinade ingredients for blending. Coarsely slice 2 stalks of lemon grass (using only 3 inches (7.5 cm) from the root end). Peel 1 onion and a thumb-sized piece of fresh ginger root. Chop roughly and blend with 2 tbsp oil, 6 fl oz (150 ml) canned coconut milk, 1 tbsp salt, and 2 tbsp sugar.

5 To make the peanut gravy, coarsely chop 1 large onion, 4 cloves garlic, 2 stalks lemon grass (use 3 in (7.5 cm) from root end), 10 candlenuts (cashews or macadamias), 1 thumb-sized piece of Laos root (galingale) – optional – and 1 thumb-sized piece of fresh ginger root, peeled.

6 Place all the dry ingredients in the blender with 1 tbsp chilli powder. Mix 2 tbsp tamarind paste (or 1 tbsp lemon juice) with 1¾ pints (1 litre) water. Strain the water from the tamarind, if used, and discard the pith. Use some of the acidulated water to blend the dry ingredients until fine and smooth.

8 Thread satay sticks with 4 or 5 cubes of beef – about 2 mouthfuls. Satay sticks are palm frond skewers, but you can use metal skewers instead. Squeeze the meat around the skewer with your hand so no bits protrude. Preheat grill until very hot, or barbecue until embers are glowing.

9 Cook or barbecue satay sticks for about 5 min, basting with oil mixed with remaining marinade. Serve satay with cucumber wedges, raw onion and compressed rice cubes. Terry's easy way to compress rice – just cook boil-in-the-bag rice for 1 hour. Drain and chill in the bag, then open and cut into cubes.

Jean Conil's Onion Tart

'French vegetarian cooking is not as radical as it might sound, neither is it a gimmick for followers of the latest fad. French vegetarianism is definitely here to stay!'

So says Jean Conil who, since the 1950s, has been a leading light in a handful of visionary chefs who have been promoting a healthier way of eating without sacrificing the pleasures of the table.

'The French have always treated vegetables with more flair and respect than most other western countries. In fact we can all learn from country people; often unable to afford much meat they have long enjoyed wild plants, pulses and humble vegetables. I believe that food should be wholesome and pure, yet it should taste just as good as the best *haute cuisine*.'

Jean first came to England as Petty Officer Chef to the British Admirals. He stayed on after the war, first at the Savoy, then as Executive Chef at Fortnum & Mason, and later as Chef de Cuisine at London's exclusive Arts Club. Jean now concentrates on promoting excellence in his style of cooking, through a combination of writing and lectur-

'You needn't miss out on a single pleasure of eating just because you choose not to eat meat'

ing, and as President of the Society of Master Chefs.

Jean remembers his youth in Vendée, the 'market garden of France', with great fondness and is still influenced by the simple, country ways of using vegetables. So it is not surprising to find him arguing the merits – in terms of both health and enjoyment – of meatless dishes.

'The onion is the humblest of all vegetables. Yet it is used to enhance almost every savoury dish, and is the main ingredient in this wonderful creamy tart. The secret is to fry the onions very slowly in butter to soften but not brown, and so bring out all the natural sweetness and flavour.

'Another little tip to remember – the warmer the climate, the sweeter the onion. Spanish onions are certainly the best although Brittany onions come a close second. The Breton people often eat them as we would an apple – raw, with a hunk of bread to accompany them. Their health-giving properties are well known, and perhaps they even "keep the doctor away" – although the effect on the breath from raw onions may keep everyone else away, too!

'As a creative person I love to modify a recipe and come up with a whole range of variations, which is, after all, the pleasure of cooking. Once you've mastered the principle of the savoury custard, the vegetable you choose to flavour it with is entirely up to you: tomatoes, mushrooms and many others will be successful. Remember it is the eggs that are responsible for the tart setting properly and then adapt the recipe to suit your own tastes. You may prefer to use milk instead of cream, but I think that once you've tried my version it will be hard to resist.

'Enjoy my Onion Tart while it is still warm and your family and friends won't even notice the absence of meat. If you take your food as seriously as we French do, you'll find the evocative flavour and aroma one of life's great pleasures. After all, good food is necessary for the enjoyment of life!'

Rub 8 oz (250 g) wholemeal flour and 4 oz (125 g) vegetable margarine together in a bowl to form a breadcrumb-like consistency. Stir in 1 beaten egg, 2 tbsp water and a pinch of sea salt and mix to a soft dough. Roll the pastry into a ball and leave to rest for 30 min.

Allow the pastry to come slightly above the rim of the tin, then trim off any excess. Crimp the edge into a fluted pattern with your thumb and forefinger.

Put the grated cheese and 3 eggs into a bowl. Pour on ¼ pt (150 ml) double cream and whisk lightly. Season with freshly ground black pepper and freshly grated nutmeg. Stir the mixture into the onions.

SERVES 6

INGREDIENTS:

FOR THE PASTRY:
8 oz (250 g) wholemeal flour
4 oz (125 g) vegetable margarine
1 egg
pinch of sea salt
FOR THE FILLING:
1 large Spanish onion, about 8 oz (250 g)
4 oz (125 g) Gruyère cheese
4 oz (125 g) mixed butter and oil
3 eggs
¼ pt (150 ml) double cream
freshly ground black pepper
freshly grated nutmeg
black olives, to garnish

2 Roll out the rested pastry to ¼in (5mm) thickness on a lightly floured surface. Grease a 2in (5cm) deep, 8in (20cm) diameter fluted, loose-bottomed flan tin.

3 Lift the pastry over the rolling pin and ease into the flan tin. Press the pastry into the base and fluted sides of the tin with your fingertips.

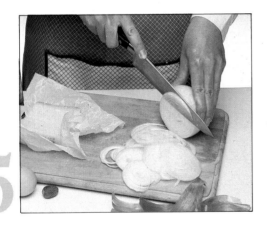

5 Peel 1 large Spanish onion, about 8oz (250g), but do not cut off the root end. Grip the onion by the root and cut across into thin slices. Grate 4oz (125g) Gruyère cheese.

6 Heat 4oz (125g) mixed butter and oil in a saucepan until the butter has melted and is sizzling. Add the sliced onion and fry gently for 8min without browning. Remove pan from the heat.

8 Pour the filling into the pastry case and cook in a preheated oven, Gas mark 6, 400°F, 200°C, for 30min until the filling is set and golden brown.

9 To remove from the tin, stand the cooked tart on a storage jar. Loosen the top edge of the pastry with a small knife and let the flan ring drop away. Slide a knife between the tin base and the tart and slip it on to a serving plate. Serve warm garnished with black olives.

John Tovey's Marbled Meat Terrine

'Entertaining is an art. Whether it is in the kitchen or the theatre, you need the same ingredients – good props, a good script and time spent setting the scene so that you can delight in the pleasure of your audience.'

John Tovey, a self-taught cook, opened Miller Howe, his highly regarded restaurant at Windermere in the Lake District, 15 years ago. Before that he ran a theatrical company, which explains why at Miller Howe dinner is an almost theatrical experience, with imaginative and carefully orchestrated menus, served amid beautiful lakeland scenery.

Out of season, John and his team travel the world promoting British food and proving that British cooking is *not* overcooked beef and soggy cabbage. John is an unashamed champion of good food. 'But, cooking and entertaining should be pleasures shared by all concerned, and that includes the cook/host too!

'I like terrines because, despite their stunning appearance, there are no complicated stages involved and they're easy to put together. It's wrong to think you've got to use

'Stunning but simple – a pleasure for the cook and the cooked-for!'

expensive meats: it's much better to use cheaper meats and marinate them expensively! Also, a terrine improves with keeping, so you can marinate at the start of the week, cook it midweek and it will be nicely matured ready for the weekend. All you have to remember is to start well in advance. The marinating takes two days and I find it's best to leave the terrine at least 24 hours after cooking to firm before slicing. It will keep for seven to eight days in the fridge or in the freezer for a month.

'Marinating is a very important stage – it breaks down the connective tissues in meat, making it more tender and adding flavour. Marinating for two days or so means that the flavour gets right through to the centre of the meat. You can do it overnight, but you won't get the same depth of flavour. At Miller Howe, we marinate a lot – as well as meat for terrines, we get loins of pork and marinate them for a week in coconut milk, halibut for a day in yogurt, and veal for a week in yogurt and peppercorns.

'I serve this Marbled Meat Terrine as a light lunch with tiny tomatoes, spring onions and crusty bread. Or, when I'm entertaining and serve it as a starter, I spoon a little mango purée over a plate and arrange a slice of terrine on top. The combination of fruit and meat is stunning.

'To serve the terrine, remove it from the fridge and allow it to come to room temperature several hours before required, as chilling dulls flavours. Cut it into thick slices with a serrated knife – dipped in hot water and used in a sawing motion, the knife will glide through.

'We always have a terrine ready for Christmas. It's just perfect for that sort of unpredictable entertaining, as you can keep going back to it. People think it's tricky, but all you need is a little imagination. You can go really over the top – adding strips of red and green pepper, asparagus spears, stuffed olives, hazelnuts and toasted almonds – so that when you cut into it you get a Picasso of colour and a titillation of tastes on the plate!'

SERVES 15
INGREDIENTS:

1 lb (500 g) boneless breast of duck
6 tablespoons port
8 oz (250 g) boneless breast of turkey or chicken
2 tablespoons cooking brandy
2 tablespoons sultanas
2 tablespoons sherry
14 oz (425 g) smoked streaky bacon rashers
8 oz (250 g) pork back fat
6 oz (175 g) belly pork meat
6 oz (175 g) lean uncooked ham
2 eggs
1/4 pt (150 ml) double cream
4 oz (125 g) shelled pistachio nuts
salt and freshly ground black pepper
4 oz (125 g) finely chopped fresh parsley

Cut 1 lb (500 g) boneless breast of duck into long thin strips, discarding skin. Place in a shallow glass dish with 6 tbsp port, cover and *marinate for 2 days* in the fridge. You can substitute pigeon or pheasant for the duck and marinate in the same way.

Drain the meats and reserve the liquids. Process 8 oz (250 g) pork back fat, 6 oz (175 g) belly pork meat, 6 oz (175 g) ham, 2 eggs, 1/4 pt (150 ml) cream and the marinade in a food processor, until well mixed. Or, put meats and fat through a mincer twice, then beat in marinade, then eggs and cream.

Line the base of the bacon-lined terrine with some of the processed mixture, arrange a layer of the parsley-coated strips over and press down lightly. Cover with more processed mixture, top with coated strips. Continue until you have used up all ingredients, finishing with a layer of the processed mixture.

Cut 8 oz (250 g) boneless breast of turkey or chicken into long thin strips, discarding skin. Place in a shallow glass dish with 2 tbsp cooking brandy and *marinate for 2 days* in the fridge. Put 2 tbsp sultanas in 2 tbsp sherry and *marinate for 2 days*.

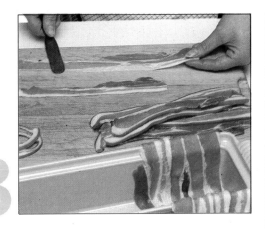

Remove rind from 14 oz (425 g) smoked streaky bacon rashers. Stretch the rashers with the back of a small knife and use to line a 14 × 3 × 3 in (35 × 7.5 × 7.5 cm) terrine, crossways, overlapping each rasher and allowing enough hanging over the edge to fold over the top. Do not line the ends of the terrine.

Skin 4 oz (125 g) shelled pistachio nuts by placing in a small bowl of boiling water. Leave to soak for 1 min, drain and peel away skins. Tip the processed mixture into a bowl, stir in the pistachios, the marinated sultanas and any liquid. Season well with freshly ground black pepper and a little salt.

Spread 4 oz (125 g) finely chopped parsley on a large plate. Roll the strips of duck and turkey or chicken breast, one at a time, in the parsley, until evenly coated.

Fold the ends of the bacon rashers over the top of the terrine to cover it completely. Cover with foil and seal edges together tightly, cover with a lid. Cook at Gas mark 4, 350°F, 180°C for 1¾ hours until firm.

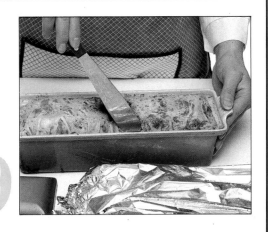

Cool, then chill for several hours. Remove lid and foil from terrine. Run a palette knife around the edge, turn the terrine out on to foil. Wrap closely and seal edges together well. *Chill for up to 48 hours* so that the terrine firms up. Allow to come to room temperature before slicing and serving.

Julia Child's Cheese Soufflé

'The Lady with the Ladle' – that was Julia Child's nickname in the mid-1960s, when she became a household name in the USA. So famous were her cookery demonstrations on television that in 1966 she won a coveted Emmy award. She became the most influential cookery teacher in the USA, bringing her speciality, French cuisine, to the tables of thousands of viewers.

In those black-and-white days, the shows were, she says, produced on such a low budget that there was only one rehearsal before taping – and her failures and faux pas were legendary! When a potato pancake fell on to the work surface, she simply scooped it back into the pan, batted her eyelids at the camera and advised, 'Remember, you're all alone in the kitchen and no one can see you.'

As a result of her years of experience, Julia Child writes her recipes honestly and vividly, inspiring confidence in the most timid of cooks. She says, 'So many people are afraid of making a soufflé – it's the timing, I'm sure. But you can *control* the timing. Although you cannot delay more than a few minutes at the serving time, you may

'A soufflé, in sooth, is mostly hot air – a thick sauce or purée, into which you fold stiffly beaten egg whites. Why then are so many people afraid of soufflés?'

assemble your soufflé as much as two hours in advance.

'Another reason for fear is lack of experience. One has not beaten enough egg whites into stiff peaks, nor folded them rapidly and delicately and often enough into a base so they retain their maximum puff. But if you've done cakes, you can do soufflés, and there's nothing truer than the old adage of "Where there's a will, there's a way". *Make the decision to conquer your fears now, and you will be Master of the soufflé.* These rules should launch you for life.

'Since the fundamental parts of a soufflé are the sauce and the egg whites, these elements need special care. A roux is the key to a successful sauce base. It takes only 2 or 3 minutes to cook flour and butter together (that is what constitutes a roux) and since there is nothing difficult about it whatsoever, there is no excuse at all for a badly made sauce. Why then do so many recipes read: melt butter, blend in flour, then beat in liquid? Why? Are we too lazy to stir flour and butter over a moderate heat for 2 to 3 minutes? Follow the method in steps 3 and 4 to produce a perfect, smooth sauce. Do not add the cheese at this stage; folding the cheese into the sauce *together with* the egg whites makes for a lighter soufflé.

'The best bowl for beating egg whites should be of such a shape that the whole mass of egg white will be in motion at once; so the bowl should not be too wide, and it should have a rounded bottom. Stainless steel or tinned metal (or, of course, hammered copper) is best. Porcelain or glass bowls allow the beaten egg whites to fall down their slippery sides, and lose volume. The bowl and whisk should be spotlessly clean – any drop of grease will prevent the egg whites from whisking properly. Electric beaters are very efficient – but so too are balloon whisks.

'Folding the egg whites into the soufflé is the key to success. Step 7 shows you how. If you have beaten your egg whites perfectly yet have trouble making your soufflé or cakes rise, it is very probable that you have not attacked the folding in with enough exuberant abandon – it needs big, rapid movements.'

INGREDIENTS:

TO PREPARE DISH:	
butter for greasing	
2 tablespoons grated cheese	
FOR THE MIXTURE:	
2 oz (50 g) Gruyère cheese	
1 oz (25 g) butter	
2 tablespoons plain flour	
salt	
white pepper	
pinch of cayenne pepper	
pinch of grated nutmeg	
6 fl oz (175 ml) hot milk	
3 eggs	
1 egg white	
1/4 teaspoon cream of tartar	

1 Preheat oven to Gas mark 6, 400°F, 200°C. Smear the inside of a 2 pt (1 litre) soufflé dish with a knob of soft butter. Coat the interior with 2 tbsp finely grated cheese. Butter a double strip of foil and wrap around the outside of the dish, making a collar that sticks 3 in (7 cm) above its rim; pin or tie in place.

4 Remove pan from heat. Immediately, start separating 3 eggs, placing the whites into a stainless steel beating bowl, and beating the yolks one by one into the hot sauce.

7 Combine the remaining egg whites and sauce by plunging your rubber spatula into the centre bottom of the pan or bowl; rapidly draw it to one side as you turn it and lift it out. Reserving 1 tbsp cheese, sprinkle in remainder with each fold of the spatula. The whole folding operation should not take more than a minute.

2 Melt 1 oz (25 g) butter in a large, heavy-based saucepan over a moderate heat. Blend in 2 tbsp plain flour and stir together for 2 min, without burning. Remove pan from heat and let it cool for a moment. Stir in ¼ tsp salt, and several grinds of white pepper, a pinch of cayenne pepper and a pinch of grated nutmeg.

3 Pour in 6 fl oz (175 ml) hot milk, all at once, vigorously beating with a wire whisk to blend perfectly. With a wooden spoon or a rubber spatula, scrape round the pan so all the roux is absorbed; beat again for a few seconds. Replace pan over heat and bring to the boil, stirring rather slowly. Boil, slowly stirring, for 2 min.

5 Add 1 extra egg white to the 3 already in the beating bowl. Start beating rather slowly until the egg whites are foaming then beat in a scant ¼ tsp cream of tartar and a pinch of salt. Gradually increase speed to fast, and continue beating until they are smooth, satiny and forming shining peaks. Do not overbeat.

6 Immediately stir a quarter of the egg whites into the warm sauce base with a rubber spatula. This will help to lighten the mixture. Scoop the rest of the egg whites on top of the sauce or pour the sauce down the side of the egg white bowl if your saucepan is not big enough for easy folding.

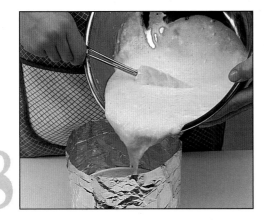

8 Scoop the soufflé mixture into the prepared dish, which should be about three-quarters filled. If you are not ready to bake the soufflé, cover with a large bowl. It can sit safely for up to 2 hours. Place the soufflé just below the centre of the preheated oven. Lower the temperature to Gas mark 5, 375°F, 190°C.

9 Do not open the oven door for 30 min. Then take a quick peek — the soufflé should have risen and the top be browned. Rapidly sprinkle on the reserved cheese and bake for a further 10 to 12 min. The soufflé is done when a skewer plunged through the side comes out almost clean. Quickly remove the collar.

Colin Spencer's Spinach Roulade

Colin Spencer discovered the wonderful adaptability of roulades as soon as he started writing 'alternative food' recipes.

'I'm dedicated to taking vegetarian food out of the sandals-and-nut-cutlets image into a gourmet cuisine in its own right. Roulades give me such a chance to contrast flavour and texture between the airy-light roll and the filling. And they are visually stunning. I soon found that when I served spectacular-looking dishes like this guests just never noticed that they were at a vegetarian party.'

Colin stopped eating all 'factory-farmed' food when he discovered that 40 per cent of the world's grain goes to feed animals for meat production. He still eats fish, though, as it's wild 'food'. His home-made taramasalata roulade filling is, he says, also superb on its own with brown bread. 'I've found that there's no need to skin the cod's roe if you have a good processor. This makes it an economical recipe, even though I don't add oil or breadcrumbs which I think blur the taste. It's strong in flavour, so spread sparingly. Do serve my roulade with the special sauce as it's a good foil.'

'A sensation on the palate of difference and distinction – and amazingly pretty'

Colin thinks this roulade makes an ideal party starter. 'It can be prepared well beforehand, but do not bake it until the day it's served. You can't taste food that's too hot or too cold; so don't chill the roulade, serve it at room temperature.

'Vegetarians have a specially keen appreciation of tastes. I like to use spinach straight from the garden – plants start losing vitamins as soon as they're picked. When buying spinach, choose fresh young leaves – not old, dark-leaved spinach. Cod's roe varies greatly: buy the darkest you can find that is still soft. I composed the recipe with a combination of cheeses: Gruyère for its melting quality, and Parmesan for its strong, clear taste. I believe all convenience foods containing additives impair the quality of my cooking.' If you find the pink peppercorns difficult to find, the green ones will do very well instead.

'You won't find roulades hard to make. The main thing is to get plenty of air into the egg whites – I always used chilled ones and a big balloon whisk to help me achieve greater volume – and try not to lose air when folding in. Check after seven to eight minutes of cooking to see if the roulade is firm – don't overcook it.

'Slice the roulade thinly – thick slices look gross – and decorate the plates with some fresh green herbs at the last moment so that they look even more stunning.'

SERVES 8
INGREDIENTS:
FOR THE TARAMASALATA:

1 lemon
4 oz (125 g) smoked cod's roe
½ small garlic clove
4 oz (125 g) cream cheese
FOR THE ROULADE:
1 lb (500 g) fresh spinach
4 eggs
2 oz (50 g) Parmesan cheese
1 oz (25 g) Gruyère cheese
¼ teaspoon ground nutmeg
¼ teaspoon ground black pepper
FOR THE SAUCE:
9 oz (275 g) Greek strained yogurt
2 tbsp pink (or green) peppercorns in vinegar
fresh chervil, to garnish

Grate rind from 1 lemon and reserve. To make taramasalata: roughly chop 4 oz (125 g) smoked cod's roe, including skin. Crush ½ small clove of garlic and put in a processor with juice of 1 lemon, 4 oz (125 g) cream cheese. Transfer taramasalata to a bowl, cover and chill.

Put spinach in a processor. Separate 4 eggs. Refrigerate whites, add yolks to spinach and process. Grate 1 oz (25 g) each fresh Parmesan and Gruyère. Gradually add to processor while running and continue until smooth. Season with nutmeg and black pepper. Transfer to a large bowl.

Trim away excess greaseproof paper from sides of roulade with scissors. This will prevent tearing and spoiling roulade. Carefully peel away paper, turning it back on itself and easing it away with the back of a knife. Trim the roulade to neaten the edges.

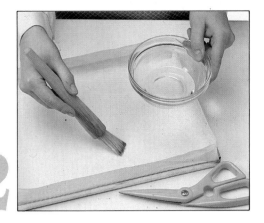

Cut a piece of greaseproof paper 1 in (2.5 cm) larger all round than a 9 × 13 in (23 × 33 cm) Swiss roll tin. Make a diagonal cut into corners. Put paper in the tin and crease the bottom edges. Overlap the corners to make a case that stands ½ in (1 cm) above the rim of tin. Brush lightly but evenly with oil.

To make the roulade: remove stalks from 1 lb (500 g) fresh spinach. Rinse leaves thoroughly. Put in a large pan, with only the water that clings to them. Cover and cook over a low heat for 10 min, shaking pan occasionally. Remove lid and increase heat, stir until the spinach appears dry.

In another large bowl, whisk egg whites to soft peaks. Using a metal spoon, mix 1 tbsp egg white into spinach mixture. Fold in remainder gently. Spoon into tin, spread gently in an even layer. Cook in an oven preheated to Gas mark 5, 375°F, 190°C, for 8–10 min until dry and is just firm to touch.

Spread a sheet of greaseproof paper on a clean tea towel. Grate 1 oz (25 g) Parmesan cheese over. Carefully invert the roulade on to the cheese. Remove tin and leave roulade to cool for 5 min.

Spread the taramasalata over roulade with a palette knife leaving a ½ in (1 cm) border at the sides and 1½ in (4 cm) at the far end uncovered. Make a shallow cut 1 in (2.5 cm) in from the short edge nearest to you. Using greaseproof for support, roll up roulade. Lift on to a plate with join underneath.

Stir reserved lemon rind into 9 oz (275 g) Greek strained yogurt. Lightly crush 2 tbsp pink peppercorns, drained from their vinegar, and stir most of them into the yogurt. Sprinkle the rest on top. Garnish roulade with fresh chervil and serve in slices, with a spoonful of sauce.

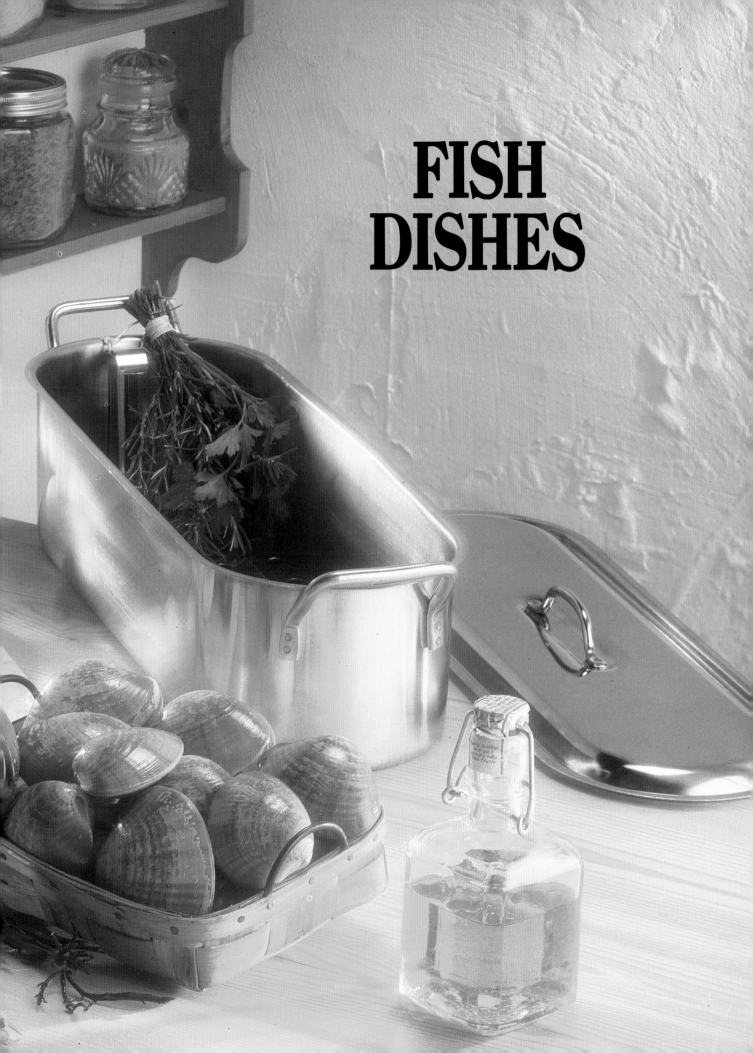

FISH
DISHES

Jane Grigson's Whole Salmon

Jane Grigson must be one of the most enthusiastic of British food writers. Her knowledge about all aspects of cooking is overwhelming, and her witty, informative style of writing makes reading a delicious experience.

'One of my most vivid memories of the Three Choirs Festival at Gloucester many years ago isn't the music but the spectacle of a huge, whole boiled salmon consumed at a lunch party. It came from the Severn or Wye and tasted marvellous... must have been agony to cook.

'Nowadays, we needn't have the worry of losing flavour to water or bouillon in an enormous fish kettle, nor of the fish becoming too dry; we can just wrap it in foil. A whole salmon cooked this way makes a beautiful summer dish, the only snag being that it should be made the day it is to be eaten, which can cause problems of organization. My advice is to keep large fish for the evening so they have time to cool, to cut down on the decor and concentrate on the ingredients.

'There's more fresh Scottish salmon available now than ever before. That's because there's a good supply of farm-

'Few of us have a fish kettle, but foil solves the problem of cooking so large a fish'

reared salmon of consistently high quality. Salmon trout – a sea-going variety of our native brown trout but with far better flavour and texture – is an excellent alternative to salmon. Sea trout is the official name, but salmon trout is what it's known by, and I'm sure this name will stick because it describes the excellence of the fish so well.

'If you don't want to buy a whole salmon, choose the moister and better flavoured tail-piece. Whatever salmon you buy, the thing is to have as large a surface area of skin as possible. This helps to lubricate and protect the salmon as it cooks. It's best to bear in mind when working out the cooking time that the thickness of the fish should be more of a guide than the weight alone.'

Jane recommends you count the number of different kinds of fish for sale. 'And count the number of different kinds you have eaten in the last few months. You may then agree that fish is one of the great untapped areas of exploration – both for curiosity and for the delight of the cook and her family and friends.

'Salmon is, to man at least, the king of fish. Much of the salmon's life history is unknown and mysterious. Its taste is so fastidious that it can only survive in pure waters. It spends most of its life in sea water, but returns to the rivers to spawn – and to be caught! They gather in the estuary, fine, fat fish in prime condition, and make their way upstream, sometimes with those immense leaps that have given the salmon the name of *Salmo salar*, the leaper.

'King as he may be, salmon is sometimes dry in his thicker portion. And all the cook's art is directed at balancing this tendency with unctuous sauces made of egg yolks, butter, cream or oil – frequently mayonnaise, but Montpellier butter is nice for a change.

'A final tip – if you don't have a serving dish long enough for a whole salmon, an attractive alternative is to invest in a piece of hardwood and oil it nicely.'

SERVES 12
INGREDIENTS:

1 × 5 lb (2.25 kg) salmon
corn oil
rock salt
freshly ground black pepper
FOR MONTPELLIER BUTTER:
4 oz (125 g) fresh herbs, spinach and watercress
1 heaped teaspoon chopped shallots
4 to 5 anchovy fillets
1 tablespoon capers
1 or 2 pickled gherkins
yolks of 3 hard-boiled eggs
1 raw egg yolk
2 fl oz (50 ml) olive oil
a little lemon juice
TO GARNISH:
1 black olive
shredded round lettuce
zest of 1 lemon

Choose a fresh, good quality salmon; have it cleaned and make a note of the weight. If the salmon is too long to fit in the oven, you'll need to cut it into pieces. With this 5 lb (2.25 kg) fish, cutting off the head is sufficient, but larger fish may have to be cut in half.

Put the two parcels on a baking tray. Cook whole fish, or pieces up to 5 lb (2.25 kg) in the centre of the oven for 1 hour; allow 12 min per lb (500 g) for pieces or whole fish over 5 lb (2.25 kg). Remove from oven, leave in sealed parcel until completely cold.

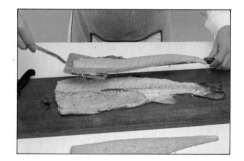

The next step is to raise the fillets. Cut along central line first and carefully slip the knife under the flesh to separate it from the bone. Slide a palette knife and a fish slice under the fillet, lift away and place on work surface. Remove next fillet in the same way.

Assemble 4 oz (125 g) fresh herbs in equal quantities, (parsley, chervil, chives, tarragon, plus spinach and watercress). Put them, with a heaped teaspoon of chopped shallot, into boiling water for 1 min. Drain well and dry.

2

Cut a piece of foil large enough to wrap the fish loosely. Make 2 foil straps to help support the weight. Place across foil. Brush with corn oil and season well. Place fish on top.

3

Put the fish head on to another sheet of oiled, seasoned foil – you won't need the straps to support it. Prepare a cool oven, Gas mark 2, 300°F, 150°C. Wrap foil round both pieces of fish to make baggy parcels. Fold and seal edges tightly.

5

Unwrap the fish pieces. Use straps to lift on to damp greaseproof on a tray. Run a sharp knife through skin down back and across tail; pull gently away from flesh, working towards head end. Turn over and remove skin from other side.

6

Now carefully scrape away the brown to expose the 'salmon pink' flesh underneath. Turn the fish on to the serving dish or board (leaving enough room for head) and prepare the other side in the same way.

8

Snip the backbone just in front of the tail with strong, sharp scissors. Slip the knife under the bone to ease it away from the bottom fillets. Pick out any remaining fine bones.

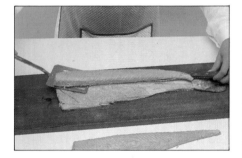

9

Using the tip of a sharp knife, remove the fins from each piece of the fish. Lift the top fillets on the palette knife and fish slice and replace them on the bottom fillets, positioning them close together.

11

Blend herbs in a liquidizer, with 4 to 5 anchovy fillets, 1 tbsp capers, 1 or 2 pickled gherkins, 3 hard-boiled egg yolks and 1 raw egg yolk. Transfer to a bowl, and beat in, drop by drop, 2 fl oz (50 ml) olive oil. Season finally with a little lemon juice.

12

Replace the fish head, covering the eye with a slice of black olive. Mask the join with discreet garnish – a little shredded lettuce and lemon zest. Serve with the Montpellier butter.

Susan Hicks's Fish Pie

Over twenty years ago, Susan Hicks went on holiday to the Scilly Isles, loved it, and moved there 'away from it all'. But when she had brought up her two children, she found herself back in the bright lights. She was spotted by a television producer and started a new and very exciting career as a television cook with her own series, *The Fish Course*, on BBC2.

Sue's expertise with fish is based firmly on experience. 'At home in the Scilly Isles fish is our basic ingredient,' she says. 'Fish is versatile, and if a recipe calls for something expensive or unavailable – swap! For my fish pie you could use smoked ling, smoked cod cutlets or Arbroath Smokies instead of smoked haddock.

'I love fish pie but, like many seemingly simple dishes, it is a test of a good cook. So often people make it an excuse for using up leftovers, or use a glutinous sauce or, worst of all, boil the fish to death. Fish pie needs care at all stages and the best, freshest ingredients to get perfect results.

'Fish should never be treated harshly. If you cook it in boiling liquid the flesh will break up and become tough.

'So easy to eat and a complete nutritional package, too – fish pie is a classic comforting, homely dish'

FISH PIE

Don't even simmer if this allows bubbles to form. Instead poach so that the surface of the liquid just shimmers. Your reward for this will be delicious flakes of tender fish.

'Another problem with fish pies is a blanketing layer of sloppy, sludgy, creamed potato. I think you'll prefer my layer of sliced potato with sauce and a crunchy gratin topping. It goes well with the smoked fish and the creaminess of the eggs. If you do use mash, fold in chopped parsley and spread it more thinly than usual.

'Don't be tempted to add extra flavourings. Smoked haddock is a quality fish whose light, smoky flavour permeates the dish. Of course, when cooking a bland fish like whiting, you can let fly with seasonings.

'I've used Finnan haddock as it is sold on the bone and this gives extra flavour to the sauce. If you buy smoked haddock fillet make sure it is undyed. So-called "smoked haddock" is sometimes just dipped in bright yellow dye, which gives no flavour or preserving effect.

'Fish is low in fat and my pie makes a healthy family meal. I use butter for the sauce as it has better flavour and cheese for the topping, but I use skimmed milk to cut down on fat where it has no purpose. Serve the pie with a fresh green salad or seasonal greens, cut into ribbon strips then lightly steamed.

'I love this dish on a wintry evening. You can prepare it in advance, and wash up the pans. Then sit down to a leisurely drink while it is cooking, knowing that when you announce to your family that you've made fish pie, their hearts will melt!'

SERVES 6
INGREDIENTS:

1½ lb (750 g) Finnan haddock
¾ pt (450 ml) semi-skimmed milk
½ lemon, sliced
1 lb (500 g) even-sized potatoes
2 large onions
2½ oz (65 g) butter
1½ oz (40 g) plain flour
salt and freshly ground black pepper
2 hard-boiled eggs
2 oz (50 g) Cheddar cheese
2 oz (50 g) fresh breadcrumbs

Place 1½ lb (750 g) Finnan haddock in a large frying pan, trimming tail off if fish is too large. Pour over ¾ pt (450 ml) semi-skimmed milk and add ½ lemon. Gently heat so milk 'shimmers', and cook for 4 min. Test by inserting a knife under the backbone. It should lift away from the flesh easily. Cool slightly.

Lift the fish away from top of backbone with a knife. Peel away backbone and discard. Separate fish into large flakes using a knife and fork. Discard the skin and any stray bones.

Spread onions in the bottom of a 3 pt (1.5 litre) shallow ovenproof dish. Spoon flaked fish over. Shell and roughly chop 2 hard-boiled eggs and place on top. Pour half the sauce over to cover evenly.

Scrub 1 lb (500 g) even-sized potatoes and slice thinly. Cook in boiling, lightly salted water for 5 min until just tender. Drain, taking care not to break the slices, and set aside.

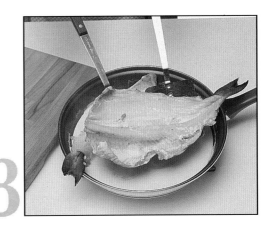

Carefully lift the fish from the frying pan with two fish slices so that it does not break up. Drain well and transfer to a chopping board. Reserve the poaching liquid for the sauce.

Slice 2 large onions thinly. Heat 1 oz (25 g) butter in a saucepan, add the onions and fry for 5 min until softened and transparent. Lift out with a slotted spoon and reserve.

Add remaining 1½ oz (40 g) butter to saucepan and heat gently until melted. Stir in 1½ oz (40 g) plain flour and mix well. Cook for 1 min. Strain reserved poaching liquid and gradually add to saucepan. Bring to the boil, stirring constantly to make a smooth creamy sauce. Season to taste with freshly ground black pepper.

Arrange the cooked potato slices neatly on top of the fish mixture so they completely cover it.

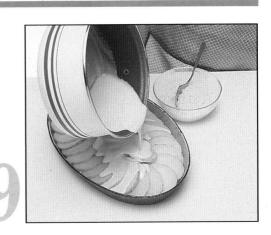

Pour the remaining sauce over the potatoes to cover them completely. Grate 2 oz (50 g) Cheddar cheese finely and mix with 2 oz (50 g) fresh breadcrumbs. Scatter over the pie and cook at Gas mark 5, 375°F, 190°C, for 20 to 30 min until the topping is golden brown.

Elisabeth Lambert Ortiz's Tempura

Japanese style currently has a strong influence in the West. Those stunningly pretty arrangements of food, thought of as *'nouvelle cuisine'*, were inspired by the spare, perfectionist style of Japanese food presentation. Yet one of Japan's most famous dishes, reveals author Elisabeth Lambert Ortiz, was originally a fish-and-chips-style dish introduced there by Portuguese traders. The Japanese elevated the dish to their own standards, inventing a light, frothy batter, diversifying the ingredients and adding a dipping sauce. They call it 'tempura'.

'It's essential to follow the recipe precisely or you'll end up with the European dish again,' explains Elisabeth. 'The Japanese sometimes sound fussy and over-exact but I found there is always a practical reason. Cut all food as directed and it will cook properly, in the time given.'

Elisabeth learned about Japanese cooking during a five-year stay in Japan with her husband, a United Nations official. She found the Japanese an intriguing mixture: very precise on some points of cooking but flexible, too. 'For instance you can use scallops instead of squid,

'Delicate batter-coated morsels to dip into a mouth-tingling sauce'

ordinary prawns instead of giant ones and spring onions or celery if some vegetables aren't in season. If you use the special ingredients like *mirin* and *bonito* flakes they give a characteristic Japanese taste.

'The secret of successful tempura is to make the batter at the last moment and to mix it lightly. Be careful not to overcrowd the pan when frying, because you need a high temperature for crisp batter. The Japanese use a tempura pan with a built-in grid for draining as they hate greasy food, but you can use an electric fryer or any deep, heavy-based pan as long as you drain really well.

'Prepare all the ingredients beforehand if you prefer to, but cook at the last moment. Tempura is a complete meal of fish and vegetables and serves as an introduction to a super new range of tastes.'

SERVES 4
INGREDIENTS:
8 large uncooked, unpeeled prawns
8 oz (250 g) prepared squid
4 oz (125 g) sole fillet
1 large carrot
12 dwarf beans
4 medium-sized flat mushrooms
1 green pepper
1 small aubergine
1 × 8 in (20 cm) square sheet dried seaweed (nori)

FOR THE DIPPING SAUCE:
2 in (5 cm) slice of white radish (mooli)
3⁄4 in (2 cm) piece root ginger
2 fl oz (50 ml) sweet rice wine (mirin) or sweet sherry
6 fl oz (175 ml) soy sauce
1 × 1⁄4 oz (5 g) packet dried tuna fish flakes (bonito—optional)
pinch of monosodium glutamate (aji-ni-moto—optional)

FOR THE BATTER:
1 egg, size 2
4 oz (125 g) plain flour
oil for deep frying

1 Remove heads from 8 large uncooked, unpeeled prawns, peel, leaving last segment of tail on and trim off wavy fringed end to tail. Make a small shallow slit on the inner edge of each prawn near the head to prevent them curling. Remove black vein.

4 Slice top off 1 green pepper and scoop out seeds. Cut in half lengthways and then into strips about 1 × 2 in (2.5 × 5 cm). Trim and slice 1 small aubergine lengthways, cut each slice across into strips about 1 in (2.5 cm) wide.

7 Bring 2 fl oz (50 ml) sweet rice wine (*mirin*) to the boil. Add 6 fl oz (175 ml) soy sauce, 6 fl oz (175 ml) water and a 1⁄4 oz (5 g) packet dried tuna fish flakes (*bonito*), stir and bring back to the boil. Add a pinch of monosodium glutamate and stir well.

10 Cook the prawns for 2 min until the batter is pale golden and bubbly. Drain well on kitchen paper or the rack of the tempura pan, and keep hot. Cook all the fish in small batches, and keep hot. Skim the oil with a draining spoon and remove any batter.

2 Rinse 8 oz (250 g) prepared squid and pat dry. Slide a knife inside each squid tube, cut in half and open out flat. Score the outside in a criss-cross pattern. Cut into 1½ in (4 cm) squares. Cut 4 oz (125 g) sole fillet into four 1½ in (4 cm) squares. Pat dry.

3 Cut a 3 in (7 cm) length from 1 large carrot and scrape sides. Cut in thin slices then into sticks. Trim 12 dwarf beans and cut into two or three diagonal slices. Wipe the caps of 4 medium-sized flat mushrooms, twist out and discard stems.

5 Cut an 8 in (20 cm) square sheet of dried seaweed (*nori*) into 1 in (2.5 cm) squares. Arrange prawns, squid and sole in 4 separate piles on a tray or plate. Arrange carrots and beans in small bundles and continue arranging the prepared ingredients in rows.

6 Cut a 2 in (5 cm) length from 1 white radish (*mooli*). Grate finely then dry between 2 sheets of kitchen paper. Divide into 4 portions. Peel ¾ in (2 cm) piece root ginger and grate finely. Divide into 4 portions.

8 When ready to cook, prepare the batter. Break a size 2 egg into a bowl, add 4 fl oz (125 ml) water and mix until smooth but not frothy. Gradually add 4 oz (125 g) sifted plain flour, mixing well. Don't worry about tiny lumps.

9 Pour 2 to 3 in (5 to 7.5 cm) oil into a saucepan, tempura pan or electric deep fryer, and heat to 350°F, 180°C – bubbles will immediately form around the tips of wooden chopsticks if ready. Dip 4 prawns into the batter and fry one at a time.

11 Dip small bundles of carrots and beans into the batter, squeeze together and fry for 2 min. Continue dipping vegetables and frying in small batches; keep hot. Dip the seaweed in the batter on one side only and fry. Skim the oil between batches.

12 Arrange the tempura on 4 serving plates. Warm the soy sauce mixture, strain into 4 small serving bowls, add the grated radish and ginger and stir. Use chopsticks to dip the fish and vegetables into the sauce before eating.

Keith Floyd's Paella

'There is nothing like a yellow mountain of paella after a hard day windsurfing or lolling on the beach under a merciless sun,' dreams TV cook Keith Floyd, 'but on a more practical note, it's an ideal party supper as it's really a one-pot dish.

'A truly authentic paella is a delicious blend of golden saffron rice, beautifully cooked shellfish and cubes of rabbit flavoured with garlic and Mediterranean herbs. It's quite irresistible, but if you're tempted to lift the lid while cooking, you'll slow down the cooking process and end up with hard rice and overcooked fish. If you haven't a traditional paella pan, use a large, heavy frying pan instead. It's all right if the rice sticks to the bottom and burns a little. Bags I scrape out the dish...

'Don't cheat by precooking the rice then stirring in precooked prawns and chicken. You may, of course, vary the ingredients to suit availability and taste. Mussels are always cheap, but many people are terrified of preparing them. There really is no mystique attached. Once you've cooked them at home you'll wonder why you haven't done

'Paella captures all the wonderful flavours of the Mediterranean in one dish'

so before. They really are delicious.

'The only bore with mussels is cleaning them. However you do it, you must observe a few simple rules. Never use any cracked or open mussels, scrub them thoroughly and remove the beard. The same applies to clams, except they don't have a beard. Langoustines are the most wonderful extravagance, well worth the expense for a special supper. If you have trouble buying, look out for frozen langoustines or Dublin Bay prawns as they're sometimes called. Cheaper too! Failing that, add a few perfect, unpeeled prawns.

'I've always felt passionately about fish. Even after nearly a year of catching, cooking, eating, talking and breathing fish for my TV series, *Floyd on Fish*, I can still honestly say, hand on heart, fish is my favourite dish. Honestly.

'As a lad, I was overcome with excitement the very first time I caught a fish. It wasn't until I'd rushed home and scoured through the *The Observer Book of Fish*, that I could put a name to my catch: trout. I wasn't even shocked when my mum deep-fried it, but something inside said there was more to fish eating than deep-frying. I resolved to find out. It's nearly 20 years since I opened my first restaurant and it would take a whole book to tell the tales of the 11 or so restaurants since!'

Keith now devotes his time to writing and broadcasting. His excitement and enthusiasm are infectious, and he constantly campaigns for a greater appreciation of fish.

'As a nation we eat about 2 lb fish per household per year – that's about one and a half unidentified frying objects per person per week. Strange that we eat so little when the fishermen of this country land so much, and in such variety. There are over 50 varieties, which means you could cook fish every week of the year and not repeat a single dish! Quite a dazzling challenge.'

SERVES 6
INGREDIENTS:

50 mussels
24 clams, if available
1 small squid
1¼ lb (550 g) rabbit or chicken pieces
1 large onion
1 red pepper
4 cloves garlic
2 fl oz (50 ml) olive oil
salt and ground black pepper
12 oz (375 g) risotto rice
1 teaspoon fresh rosemary and thyme leaves
1 large pinch saffron strands
12 langoustines or Dublin Bay prawns
2 tablespoons pine nuts

Scrub 50 mussels thoroughly. Rinse under cold running water. Discard any open or cracked shells. Scrape each one free of barnacles and seaweed until they sparkle like black pearls.

Cut off the tentacles and head of 1 squid and discard. You will be left with a sort of purse. Plunge your hand into this purse and pull out the intestines.

Bone and dice 1¼ lb (550 g) rabbit or chicken pieces. Increase the quantity if you prefer them to mussels or squid. Chop 1 large onion. Cut 1 red pepper into thin strips, discarding pith and seeds. Chop 4 cloves of garlic.

Add 25 fl oz (625 ml) water, 1 tsp fresh rosemary and thyme leaves, pinch of saffron, mussels, squid and clams. Replace saffron with ½ tsp turmeric if necessary: the colour is the same but the flavour less authentic.

Rip off the fibrous beard which protrudes between the shells. Press each mussel at the join of the shells – if there's no movement it's not full of sand, so is safe to use. Discard if there *is* any movement.

Scrub 24 clams thoroughly. Discard any open or cracked shells you find.

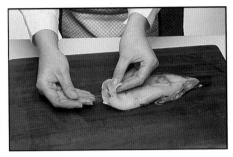

Remove the clear 'plastic' bone, which looks like a corset stay or collar stiffener.

Peel off the thin outside film. Rinse under cold running water. Cut squid into either thin rings or large rectangular shapes.

Heat 2 fl oz (50 ml) olive oil in a large iron paella or frying pan. Season rabbit or chicken with salt and ground black pepper and fry for 3 or 4 min. Add the chopped onion, red pepper and garlic and fry with the meat until golden.

Wash and drain 12 oz (375 g) rice. Add to the pan and stir well until every grain is well coated with oil and thoroughly mixed with the other ingredients. Add a little more olive oil if necessary.

Cover with a large lid or foil and cook gently over a low heat for 20 min.

Remove the lid and add 12 langoustines or Dublin Bay prawns and cook for a further 10 min. Remove any mussels or clams that haven't opened and discard. Finally, sprinkle 2 tbsp pine nuts over and serve.

Patricia Lousada's New England Fish Chowder

The cooking of America is as diverse as the variety of settlers who have arrived on her shores since the days of the Pilgrim Fathers. Adapted to prevailing conditions across this vast New World, and assimilating ingredients being used by the native Indian population, the essentially European cuisines brought across from England, France, Holland, Italy and Poland have merged and blended into a style of cooking that is uniquely American.

Fish chowder is a typical product of this cultural melting-pot. 'The name "chowder" comes from the French *la chaudière*,' explains Lady Lousada, 'the name given by Canadian and northern New England fishermen to the huge copper pot in which they cooked their communal fish stew. This was a tradition brought over from the Atlantic and Mediterranean coasts of France – celebrating the safe return of the fleet, with each fisherman contributing something from his catch for the 'chowder'. After the rigours of the fishing trip they must have welcomed such a warm, satisfying meal, too. In France the dish called *bouillabaisse* is based on the same principle – a

'This hearty, warming soup is the perfect antidote to our cold Northern climate'

complete meal cooked in one pot and based on whatever fish comes to hand. New England chowder, however, contains potatoes and salt pork too, no doubt to counteract the colder northern climate.'

Born in New York City Lady Lousada learned a great deal about Italian and French cuisine from her Italian mother, a singer and an inspired cook. Later, as a member of the New York City Ballet, Lady Lousada herself became involved in cookery in the company of her hungry fellow dancers. Two years in Paris, attending lectures at the Cordon Bleu school with 'background study' conducted in wonderful Parisian restaurants, deepened her interest still further.

She retains an abiding affection for American food, however, with memories of apple pie and toll house cookies, and the five books she has written for Sainsbury's include *American Sampler* and *The Great American Bake-in*. Living in London with an English husband and four children, her cosmopolitan cooking style is much in demand.

'Traditionally, chowder would be made with fillets and trimmings from the same fish, but it's more convenient to buy the two separately. Fish heads are particularly good for the stock, while the fillets can be from any fish with firm, white flesh. Apart from using absolutely first-rate ingredients there are no real secrets to preparing the dish – remember that both fish and potatoes are easily over-cooked, though, so it does need careful watching.'

SERVES 6
INGREDIENTS:
FOR THE STOCK:

1 tbsp butter
1 onion
1 carrot
½ stalk celery
1½ lb (750 g) fish heads, backbones and trimmings

FOR THE CHOWDER:

6 oz (175 g) salt pork or piece of unsmoked bacon
1 tbsp oil
2 lb (1 kg) onions
2 tbsp plain flour
2 lb (1 kg) potatoes
1 teaspoon freshly chopped thyme or ½ teaspoon dried thyme
1 bay leaf
1½ pints (900 ml) milk
2½ lb (1.25 kg) fresh or frozen cod, haddock or other fish fillets, all one kind or a mixture
salt
freshly ground black pepper

TO GARNISH:

8 water biscuits
chopped parsley

Melt 1 tbsp butter in a large pan and add the onion, carrot and celery, all finely chopped. Cover and sweat over gentle heat until soft, about 5 min. Add the fish head and trimmings and cook for 2 min. Add 2 pt (1.2 litres) cold water, bring to the boil, reduce heat and simmer for 20 min, uncovered. Strain and reserve.

Heat 1 tbsp oil in a large, heavy pan over moderate heat. Fry cubes of meat until they are lightly brown and fat has melted.

Peel 2 lb (1 kg) potatoes and slice thinly. Add to the pan with reserved fish stock and the herbs. Season to taste with pepper and salt if necessary – the pork can be quite salty – cover and cook over gentle heat until the potatoes are quite tender, about 10 to 15 min.

2 Meanwhile, remove the rind from 6 oz (175 g) salt pork or piece of unsmoked bacon with a sharp, pointed knife and cut meat into ½ in (1 cm) cubes. Cut 2½ lb (1.25 kg) fish fillets into 2 in (5 cm) chunks.

3 Place the cubes of meat in a saucepan containing 2 pt (1.2 litres) boiling water and blanch for 5 min. Drain thoroughly.

5 Slice 2 lb (1 kg) onions thinly and add to the pan. Cook for 8 to 10 min, stirring frequently. Do not let them burn or the colour of the finished soup will be spoiled.

6 Sprinkle over 2 tbsp plain flour and cook, still stirring, for a further 2 min.

8 Shortly before you are ready to serve the chowder, bring it to the boil and add 1½ pt (900 ml) milk. Let the chowder come back to the boil and add the chunks of fish. Reduce the heat and simmer gently for about 5 min or until the fish is just cooked.

9 To serve, pour the chowder into wide soup bowls. Break the water biscuits into small pieces and sprinkle them on top, with a little chopped parsley.

POULTRY
and
GAME

René Rochon's Coq au Vin

Chez Solange is a favourite eating place of many Londoners and visitors alike. It is here that you'll find René Rochon and his 16 kitchen staff preparing more than 70 portions of Coq au Vin every day. One lady has been coming to his restaurant every Thursday for the past 25 years to enjoy his cooking and to soak up the bustling, friendly atmosphere of this truly authentic French restaurant. René trained as a chef for many years in France before coming to England in 1951 as the *sous chef* (second in command) at the Savoy. Here he learned English – though after 33 years he still maintains his strong French accent. 'My English is lazy, but I think if I lose my French accent, my French food will not be as good!' he jokes. Embroidered on his best 'whites' are the words *Bravo à René Rochon, pour ses 50 ans de piano* – 'well done René for 50 years at the stove' (*piano* is French chefs' slang), a loving tribute from his colleagues. And after 54 years of cooking, René's Coq au Vin is consistently superb. 'It almost certainly began as a farmer's stew using farm chickens and wine from their own vineyards,' explains

'Coq au Vin is simply a stew, it takes a little time but that's all. I've been cooking it for 54 years, so really I should know!'

René. 'People don't make it at home very often because it takes a little time, but the end result makes it worthwhile.

'Coq au Vin is only as good as the ingredients that go into it. I cut a chicken into eight so each person gets a little white, and a little dark meat. Why not learn the French way to joint a chicken, especially as it is now one of the most economical and popular meats? And don't waste the carcass; boil it with some carrot, onion, bay leaf for stock. I add vermicelli to make a wonderfully simple soup.

'Use only the cheapest French red table wine for cooking. Marinating the chicken in it overnight imparts a marvellous flavour, as well as tenderizing the meat. But drink a full-bodied red wine – a Burgundy – with it!

'My wife, Thérèse, does all the cooking at home, as well as all the administration at the restaurant – named after our eldest daughter, Solange. My son Jacques runs the wine bar section, so you can see it's very much a family concern. Only Nathalie is still studying.

'I consider myself retired now – I only work seven hours a day, from 8am to 4pm! At midday I treat myself to a glass of champagne in the wine bar and chat with the customers. I like my work, I love those I work with, and I like my food. I hope to die in the kitchen watching my people working around me.'

SERVES 4
INGREDIENTS:

1 large chicken, about 4 lb (2 kg) dressed weight
2 large onions
1 carrot
1 clove garlic
1 sprig parsley
1 sprig thyme
1 bay leaf
salt and pepper
2 pt (1 litre) red French table wine
4 tablespoons flour
2 tablespoons cooking oil
4 oz (100 g) butter
4 tomatoes
1 tablespoon tomato purée
1 lb (500 g) button mushrooms
4 slices white bread
3 teaspoons butter
3 teaspoons flour

Pull one leg of chicken away from the body and cut through the skin. Bend leg right back, forcing bone out of socket. Insert tip of knife between bones and slice through flesh to remove leg. Cut through the joint between thigh and drumstick. Cut off the scaly joint at the top of the drumstick. Repeat with other leg.

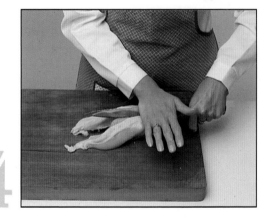

Cut the breast into two along breastbone. Place portions in a shallow, non-metallic dish. Peel and finely slice 2 onions and 1 carrot. Peel and slice 1 clove of garlic. Tie herbs with cotton for easy removal. Add to the chicken. Season and pour over 2 pt (1 litre) red wine. Cover and refrigerate for 24 hours.

Meanwhile, make bread croûtons. Remove crusts from 4 slices of white bread and cut into eight triangles. Heat about 2 oz (50 g) butter in a frying pan and fry the triangles of bread on both sides until crisp and golden. Drain on kitchen paper.

2 Cut off wings. Don't just remove the wing at the joint or it makes a mean serving. Slice through part of the breast, separating it from the body at the wing joint. Take a fair slice of breast meat on this portion so that each portion has about the same amount of meat. Repeat process with other wing. If liked, cut off wing tips.

3 Turn the chicken on to one side. Separate the fleshy part of the breast from the backbone by cutting through the thin rib bones and the membrane on each side of the bird – in effect, removing the top half of the carcass (boil the remainder with carrots, onion and bay leaf to make stock).

5 Next day, lift out chicken and drain, reserving the marinade. Pat chicken pieces dry and dust lightly with flour, salt and pepper; shake off excess. Heat 2 tbsp oil and 2 oz (50 g) butter in a large frying pan until 'hazing'. Add chicken and fry, turning frequently, until golden brown. Transfer to a flameproof casserole.

6 Skin 4 tomatoes: cover with boiling water for 2 min, then plunge them into cold water. Quarter and add to the casserole with 1 tbsp tomato purée, 1 lb (500 g) button mushrooms and marinade. Bring to the boil, cover and simmer for 15 min. Pierce legs with a skewer to check the juices are no longer bloody.

8 Make a *beurre manié*: beat together equal quantities of butter and flour to a smooth paste (in this case, for this quantity, you'll need 3 tsp butter and 3 tsp flour). Make sure the mixture is smooth, with no lumps of flour remaining. Transfer the chicken portions to a warmed serving dish, using a draining spoon.

9 Bring the liquid to the boil, and drop in small pieces of the *beurre manié* while whisking continuously. Continue until all the mixture has been added. Simmer for 15 min until the sauce has thickened to a coating consistency. Taste and adjust the seasoning. Pour the sauce over the chicken and garnish with croûtons.

Richard Olney's Boned Poached Chicken

'Elegantly glazed and decorated, boned poached chicken makes an attractive centrepiece to any buffet or summer menu,' says Richard Olney. 'You can carve it at the table in the traditional way, or carve it into cross section slices – a simple method that wastes no meat.'

Born in the USA, Richard has lived half his life in France, and has become an authority on food and wine, especially 'simple French food'. 'Good and honest cooking and good and honest French cooking are the same thing. Certainly there are national dishes, just as there are regional dishes, but it is comforting to realize that the principles of good cooking do not change as one crosses frontiers.

'The most usual way to bone a chicken is to split it the length of the back and open it out for boning, working round both sides of the carcass. But the method shown below is easily the simplest and gives the most elegant results. It's just a question of turning the chicken inside out, removing the bare carcass and turning it right side out again. For the sake of presentation, the bones of the wings

'This dish, in its presentation, lends itself to fanciful dress'

and legs are left in place, so that the cooked bird looks normal – *until it's carved*.

'The prepared bird is poached, rather than roasted, for flavour and economy. (The casserole dish should be large enough for the bird to fit in neatly without being squashed.) Covered with stock, brought slowly to a simmer, then kept at just below boiling point, the flesh stays pale, meltingly tender and juicy. Wrapping the bird in muslin or a tea towel keeps it in good shape and keeps the breast, not entirely covered by stock, moist too.

'The chicken should be prepared the day before the dinner. It may be decorated and glazed with jelly on the morning of the same day. 'If you don't want to decorate the chicken, then just cool it as in the recipe, remove the trussing string, fit it into a terrine or casserole, and pour the wine-flavoured jellied stock (see step 12) over it, leaving it to set. If you like the chicken decorated, but more jellied, put it on a large serving dish and repeatedly trickle the semi-liquid jelly over. Chill until serving.

'A perfect meal depends on many things, one of which is menu composition.' And Richard has lots of good menu planning advice to share. Essentially, the only thing to remember is that the palate should be kept fresh, teased, surprised and excited throughout the meal.

'Also, consider presentation – the eye must be flattered as well as the palate. Rustic preparations look best served directly from the earthenware vessels they were cooked in. Elegant preparations should be elegantly presented. Cold food, like this chicken, lends itself best to fanciful dress, but however presented, food should always look like food.

And Richard's recommendation to serve with the chicken? 'Tossed green salad with parsley, chervil, tarragon and chives – the classic *fines herbes*.'

SERVES 8
INGREDIENTS:

5 lb (2.25 kg) oven-ready chicken
1 onion
3 cloves
1 carrot
1 bouquet garni
few peppercorns
juice of 1 lemon
FOR THE STUFFING:
10 oz (300 g) chicken livers
1 oz (25 g) unsalted butter
large handful fresh breadcrumbs
1 clove garlic
1 teaspoon mixed dried herbs
1 tablespoon finely chopped parsley
1 finely chopped onion
2 eggs
salt and freshly ground pepper
TO GARNISH:
small glass fortified wine (Madeira, sherry, port)
tarragon leaves
canned pimiento
black olives

Place chicken on work surface, breastbone up. Lift flap of neckskin and pull it right back. Feel for wishbone with your fingers. With a small, sharp-pointed knife cut at top of wishbone, then round the entire V-shaped bone and remove it from meat.

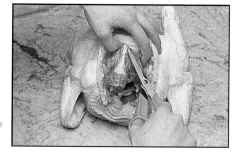

Turn chicken over, use scissors to snip meat away from backbone. Loosen halfway along the backbone until you feel the top of the spoon-shaped bones that contain the 'oysters'. Using fingers, push the meat away, and release the 'oysters'.

Cut through backbone just before tail, to leave 'parson's nose' in place. Remove carcass. Cover bones, 1 peeled onion studded with 3 cloves, 1 carrot, 1 bouquet garni, and peppercorns with water. Boil, skim, and simmer for 2 hours. Strain stock then chill.

Rub the surface of the chicken with fresh lemon juice. Wrap firmly in a double layer of muslin (or an old, clean tea towel) to keep the chicken a good shape during cooking. Tie the muslin at each end with string.

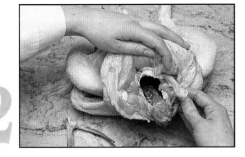

2

Feel under the breast meat for the next bone (*not* the wing bone). Expose the hinge by snipping through the tendons. Feel along the bone, pushing the flesh away. Its fatter part joins the breastbone; the thin, flat part runs downwards. Twist out together.

3

Repeat on other side, then push fingertips round top and sides of carcass to detach meat. Take care over curved front end of breastbone, as you could tear the skin. Snip through any bits you can't loosen. Clear meat from front 2 in (5 cm) of carcass.

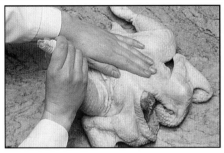

5

You won't be able to get any further until you detach the leg bones from the carcass. Turn the bird the other way up, twisting the leg until you break the ball and socket joint. Do this carefully so as not to tear the skin.

6

Turn chicken over and work along breastbone again, feeling your way. Work on breastbone (as far as you can go without tearing the skin), then backbone (as far as you can go) alternately, clearing flesh from carcass. Detach legs by snipping tendons.

8

Sew up 'parson's nose' end and make stuffing: fry 10 oz (300 g) chicken livers in 1 oz (25 g) butter until just browned. Chop finely. Add breadcrumbs. Mix in crushed garlic, 1 tsp mixed dried herbs, 1 tbsp parsley, chopped onion, 2 eggs, seasoning. Stuff chicken.

9

With chicken breast down, run trussing needle through upper part of wing, through neck skin (folded over back) and back through next wing. Turn chicken over, pull legs into place, sew through legs and body near 'knee', pull together string ends; knot.

11

Skim stock and pour over chicken in a casserole dish. Boil, reduce to a bare simmer, and poach, with lid ajar, for 1½ hours. Remove chicken and chill, wrapped. Strain liquid, cool, chill. When jellied, remove fat. If stock does not jelly, boil, then chill.

12

Unwrap chicken, remove trussing and wipe with hot cloth. Melt stock, add wine, spoon over bird and chill. Decorate with tarragon (first dipped in boiling water), pimiento and black olives, dipped in jelly. Continue spooning jelly to build up glaze: chill to set.

Judy Bastyra's Chicken Pelau

Anyone who is saving seriously for essentials shouldn't talk to writer Judy Bastyra – she makes you want to spend the lot on air tickets to the Caribbean.

'I can only say it's like entering a magical new world of heat, light and colour. Imagine opening a window in your beach house and picking a pawpaw from the tree outside! Admittedly, the first time I went there was to honeymoon at my husband's family home. But the islands and their cooking have become my passion.'

Judy's recipes were collected from friends in the course of many Caribbean trips, and they explain how to use the West Indian ingredients now widely available in Britain. 'Part of the fun of Caribbean cooking is the shopping. I love going to a lively street market and choosing from the great heaps of exotic produce. You get into conversations with the stall-holders about what you're cooking and how their auntie or granny makes it – because recipes vary from island to island. So you can add sultanas, olives, capers or peppers to this pelau. Some people always finish theirs with a splash of rum.

'Perfect for summer entertaining – interesting, exotic ingredients yet easy to make'

CHICKEN PELAU

'The three ingredients which you may find unfamiliar are pigeon peas, plantains – or cooking bananas – and the hot seasoning peppers which give an authentic West Indian taste. You'll find the latter in varying ripeness, green, yellow or red – all are fine. Don't try eating them, though, as they're added for flavouring only and would be lethally hot. Plantains are delicious fried, but you must choose ripe ones, which have black skins.

'The other really characteristic West Indian technique is the sugar-browning of meat. This gives delicious flavour and mellowness. Once you've tried it in this recipe you can sugar-brown cubed belly pork, lamb or rabbit to make an equally good, but different, pelau.

'It's a super, no-fuss recipe for when another family comes in a crowd for lunch or supper. My two children are often fussy but they love this and the fried plantains I serve with it. In the West Indies we'd enjoy it after a day on the beach as it's superb cold and it reheats well.

'I find it fascinating how history has come full circle. Pigeon peas came to the Caribbean from Africa with the slaves, rice dishes with the later Indian immigrants. Mixed-origin recipes like this are called Creole cooking over there. Now the dish has returned across the Atlantic, giving us a chance to learn from a New World culture and to enjoy a flavour that's unique to the West Indies.'

SERVES 6
INGREDIENTS:

6 oz (175 g) dried pigeon peas or black-eyed beans
2 sticks celery
1 large onion
2 garlic cloves
2 tablespoons chopped fresh chives
2 tablespoons fresh thyme leaves
1 fresh coconut
1 hot seasoning pepper (also called hot bonnet pepper) or
¼ teaspoon hot pepper sauce
3½ lb (1.6 kg) fresh or chilled chicken
5 tbsp oil
3 tablespoons granulated sugar
8 oz (250 g) long-grain rice
3 ripe plantains
1 oz (25 g) butter
grated nutmeg
caster sugar

Soak 6 oz (175 g) pigeon peas or black-eyed beans in cold water overnight or for at least 4 hours. Drain, place in a saucepan and cover with fresh water. Bring to boil and simmer for 45 min until tender. Don't overcook or they'll disintegrate. Drain.

Pierce the 'eyes' of 1 fresh coconut with a skewer. Drain the liquid into a measuring jug and make it up to ½ pt (300 ml) with water. Crack open the coconut with a hammer. Prise out the flesh from one half, peel away the brown skin and chop the flesh.

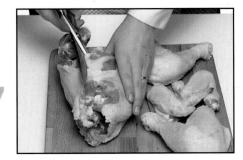

Cut wings and legs from a 3½ lb (1.6 kg) fresh or chilled chicken. Turn on to one side. Cut into body cavity at the base of the ribs and cut carcass in half. Discard the lower half. Cut breast into two portions through breast bone.

Add half the prepared chicken pieces and fry in a single layer for about 15–20 min, turning frequently until a rich deep brown all over. Lift out with a slotted spoon and reserve. Brown remaining chicken in the same way. Return to the casserole.

2 Roughly chop 2 sticks celery, 1 large onion and 2 garlic cloves. Strip enough chives to give 2 tbsp. Strip leaves from a small bunch of thyme to give 2 tbsp.

3 To make the seasoning sauce, put prepared ingredients and 4 tbsp water in a processor or blender and switch on for 30 seconds until puréed. Pour the mixture into a saucepan, scraping out any residue with a plastic spatula.

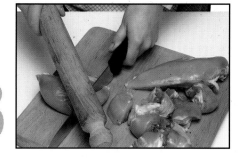

5 Purée coconut flesh in a processor or blender, gradually adding the coconut liquid. Continue processing until the mixture is finely chopped and thickly coats the back of a spoon. If it's too thick add a little extra water.

6 Add 1 whole hot seasoning pepper or ¼ teaspoon hot pepper sauce to the seasoning sauce in the pan. Add the coconut mixture and pigeon peas. Season and cook over a low heat for 15 min, stirring occasionally.

8 Remove skin from all the pieces. Cut chicken into neat 1 in (2.5 cm) pieces. To break through bones, position a large, well-sharpened knife blade on the meat and hit down on it with a rolling pin.

9 Heat 3 tbsp of the oil and 3 tbsp granulated sugar together in a large, heavy-based flameproof casserole. Cook over a moderate heat but, once sugar begins to melt, reduce heat and watch carefully – the mixture should caramelize but must not burn.

11 Stir in the coconut mixture, rice and ½ pt (300 ml) water. Season. Bring to the boil, reduce heat to low and cover tightly. Simmer for 15 min, or until the chicken is tender and the rice has absorbed all the liquid. Discard pepper.

12 Peel plantains and cut into 3 lengths. Cut lengthways into thin slices. Fry slices a few at a time in 1 oz (25 g) butter and 2 tbsp oil until browned. Drain and sprinkle with nutmeg and caster sugar. Serve pelau with plantains and tomato relish.

Gilly Cubitt's Peking Duck

'Food is an extremely important part of the Chinese way of life,' says Gilly Cubitt, *Family Circle*'s food and nutrition editor. 'A dish must do more than just taste nice – it must please the eye and provide harmonious contrasts in texture and flavour. So you'll find crispness teamed with tenderness, sweet with sour or spicy flavours, and often elaborate, meticulous presentation.

'Peking Duck is a famous example of this perfect harmony – crisp, sweet skin, and spiced succulent meat, with crunchy, moist accompaniments. And it has the bonus of economy, for traditionally, one duck is used to create three tasty, moreish courses.

'In China the dish is so highly regarded that many chefs specialize in it and restaurants cater exclusively for Peking Duck meals. For the first course you'll have the savoury-flavoured breast meat and specially crisped skin served with fresh spring onions, cool cucumber, tangy hoi-sin sauce and featherlight pancakes. The Chinese use their chopsticks to spread a little of the sauce over the pancake, which is then topped with the vegetables and meat and

'A perfect harmony of tastes, textures and colour – this classic dish is Chinese cuisine at its very best'

rolled up to eat. For the second course, the remaining meat, including thighs and wings, is shredded and stir-fried with vegetables. To finish, a rich duck soup is made from the carcass.

'But for British diners,' says Gilly, 'unless you want a particularly authentic meal, three courses of duck may be a little overwhelming! I find it easier to serve the first course only, plus a dessert. I either use all the duck in this way or just use the breast and leg meat and freeze the rest to make a stir-fry and soup later.

'The Chinese rear ducks specially for this dish, but oven-ready types work perfectly well. The secret of success lies in the fabulous crispy skin – the most prized part of Peking Duck – and the spicy powder sprinkled inside. To ensure a crisp skin, chefs will inflate the duck between skin and flesh, and you can still find recipes that suggest judicious use of a bicycle pump! I just pinch the skin all over to detach it from the meat and break up the fat.

'The bird is then scalded with boiling water to open up the pores so they readily absorb the sweet-and-sour basting liquid, placed on a rack and left overnight in a draughty place to dry.

'The five-spice powder used to flavour the cavity of the duck produces the most tantalizing, evocative aroma while cooking – something which will really tempt your guests' tastebuds! Also known as five-fragrance powder it is a blend of star anise, cloves, cinnamon, Szechwan pepper and fennel.

'Wheat flour, rather than rice, is the staple in the Peking region of China, which is probably why the dish was made with pancakes. They also contribute to the balance of the meal – the rich meat needs a contrast of plain carbohydrate as well as the crispness provided by the spring onions and cucumber and the moisture given by the hoi-sin sauce. The latter is a Chinese barbecue sauce made from red beans, chilli powder, sugar and spices. It's usually called Barbecue Sauce with 'hoi-sin' in brackets underneath.

'I first learned how to cook Peking Duck on a visit to Hong Kong,' says Gilly. 'It's since become a favourite dinner party menu; a wonderfully exotic meal prepared relatively easily.'

SERVES 4
INGREDIENTS:

5 lb (2.25 kg) oven-ready duck
3 tablespoons five-spice powder
2 teaspoons salt
5 tablespoons honey
2 tablespoons red wine vinegar
5 tablespoons white wine
FOR THE PANCAKES:
8 oz (250 g) strong plain flour
oil
TO SERVE:
1 bunch spring onions
½ cucumber
hoi-sin sauce

Rinse and dry a 5 lb (2.25 kg) oven-ready duck, put on a board and pinch the skin all over to loosen it – but take great care not to tear it.

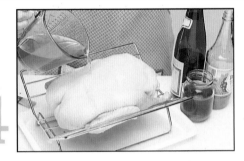

Make up basting liquid from 5 tbsp honey, 2 tbsp red wine vinegar, 5 tbsp white wine and ½ pt (300 ml) boiling water. Put the duck on a roasting tray and pour liquid over. Collect liquid and baste again. Leave in a cool, draughty place overnight.

Divide dough into 2 'sausages' about 8 in (20 cm) long. Cut each into 10 pieces and press flat with heel of hand. Flatten between hands until about 2 to 2½ in (5 to 6 cm) in diameter. Brush half the pieces lightly with oil. Sandwich with the unoiled pieces.

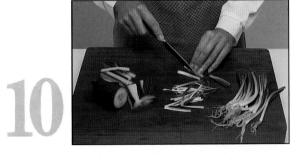

Trim 1 bunch spring onions; halve and cut into fine strips. Cut half a cucumber into thin sticks about 3 in (7 cm) long. Place in small serving bowls. Pour hoi-sin sauce into another small bowl.

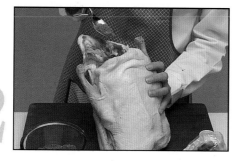

Mix 3 tbsp five-spice powder and 2 tsp salt together. Spoon into cavity, then turn duck so inside is evenly coated.

Put duck in a bowl or a colander in the sink. Pour a kettleful of boiling water over, turning duck so it is scalded all over. This makes the skin shrink and take on a dry, slightly shiny appearance.

Preheat the oven to Gas mark 5, 375°F, 190°C. Put the duck on its rack in a roasting tin. Cook for 1½ to 1¾ hours, until the juices run clear when thigh is pierced with a fine skewer.

Meanwhile, make lotus-leaf pancakes. Put 8 oz (250 g) strong plain flour into a bowl and add 6 to 7 fl oz (175 to 200 ml) boiling water, stirring well with chopsticks or a wooden spoon. Knead until smooth, then leave covered with a cloth for 20 min.

Place on a lightly floured board and roll each pair with a rolling pin, rotating dough and turning it over halfway through, until it makes an even circle about 5 in (12 cm) in diameter.

Heat a heavy-based frying pan or griddle without oil. Fry pancakes for 1 or 2 min until lightly browned in spots. Turn over and fry other side for about 30 seconds. Remove from pan and peel apart carefully. Cover with a cloth.

Cut through skin of duck between leg and breast. Pull legs away from body and sever at joint. Cut off drumsticks. Run knife around edge of skin covering breast. Remove carefully in one piece.

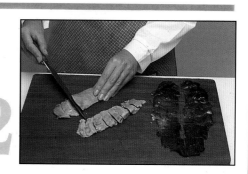

Cut the skin into neat pieces. Cut off breast fillets and slice diagonally. Cut all remaining meat off duck and arrange it on a plate with the drumsticks. Serve with vegetables and hoi-sin sauce.

The Earl of Bradford's Hot Game Pie

Ask the Earl of Bradford what his favourite food is and he will quickly answer – 'pies'. 'There's something honest and straightforward about a good old-fashioned English pie.' A statement that regular visitors to London's popular 'Porters' restaurant would agree with. Richard started the restaurant over seven years ago, just as Covent Garden was changing from a busy fruit and vegetable market to a thriving tourist area, and has never looked back. 'There's something remarkably unseasonal about a really good pie; perhaps it's something to do with our dreadful British weather!

'Although I enjoy lots of different pies, I think one of my favourites must be Hot Game Pie: moist tender pieces of venison and hare with that wonderful gamey flavour, topped with light, melt-in-the-mouth pastry layers. It always makes me think of large winter shooting parties at Weston Park, my home in Shropshire. Being outside all day in all weathers really gives one the most tremendous appetite. For large parties I make big pies but when a few friends come over for dinner I usually make the pies in

'Presentation is important but flavour more so. Good food has lots of oomph!'

individual dishes, because they're so much easier to serve.

'The secret of a truly good game pie is the inclusion of hare; it really seems to bring out the flavour. I think flavour is so important, don't you? It doesn't matter how good a dish looks, it's the flavour that counts. And it's absolutely vital to marinate the meat in red wine, as venison can sometimes be a little dry.

'I always sweat the vegetables in a mixture of butter and oil and brown the meat first, too. It's the little things that count, the smallest touch of garlic plus a dash of Worcestershire sauce makes a world of difference. I think it's important for food to have lots of oomph!

'I insist on good stock. Never throw away any bones. Brown them in a hot oven so that the stock has a good colour, then gently bubble in a large pan of water with onions, celery, carrot and thyme. Make in large, concentrated batches and then keep in the freezer. I couldn't be without my freezer. I am delighted to see that everyone can get fresh and frozen venison now.

'When cooking any game, it's important to cook the meats gently in a slow oven. If you have time I really think it's worth making the meat mixture the day before and chilling it overnight so that the flavours have a chance to mingle and develop. If cooking for friends over Christmas it is an ideal dish to freeze away so it's ready when things are really hectic. I'm a great one for cutting corners – it's really not worth making your own puff pastry, bought puff pastry is so consistently good and I honestly don't think most people can tell the difference.

'Food is such a pleasure, I really enjoy getting out in the kitchen, although I must admit my wife isn't always so keen. I find cooking so relaxing, especially with a glass of chilled white wine to hand. It's just what you need to get you in the festive spirit.'

SERVES 6
INGREDIENTS:

2 lb (1 kg) boneless lean venison
1 hare, cut into joints
sprig of thyme
½ pt (300 ml) red wine
8 rashers streaky bacon
2 tablespoons oil
1 oz (25 g) butter
8 oz (250 g) fresh or frozen baby onions
4 oz (125 g) button mushrooms
3 tablespoons plain flour
1 clove garlic, crushed
½ pt (300 ml) good beef or game stock
1 tablespoon Worcestershire sauce
salt and ground black pepper
1 lb (500 g) puff pastry, thawed if frozen
beaten egg, to glaze

With a sharp knife cut 2 lb (1 kg) boneless lean venison into large chunks, discarding any fat. Carefully take the meat off jointed hare, and cut into large chunks.

Drain meat and reserve marinade. Add meat to the pan a few pieces at a time and fry until well browned. Return all the meat to the pan and sprinkle with 3 tbsp plain flour, stir well and cook for 1 min.

Roll out 1 lb (500 g) puff pastry, thawed if frozen. Place the pie dish on the pastry and cut a pastry lid, 1 in (2.5 cm) larger than the top of the pie dish. Cut long ½ in (1 cm) wide strips and press around the wetted rim of the pie dish. Brush this with water and place the pastry lid in position, lifting it with a rolling pin.

2 Place the venison and hare in a large shallow dish with a sprig of thyme. Pour ½pt (300ml) red wine over, cover and leave to marinate in a cool place for at least 4 hours or overnight, stirring once or twice.

3 Remove the rind from 8 rashers of streaky bacon and roughly chop. Fry in 2tbsp oil and 1oz (25g) butter in a large flameproof casserole until browned. Peel 8oz (250g) fresh baby onions or use frozen. Add to pan with 4oz (125g) button mushrooms and cook for 3min. Lift out with a draining spoon and reserve.

5 Return the bacon and vegetables to the pan. Add 1 clove of garlic, crushed, ½pt (300ml) good beef or game stock and 1tbsp Worcestershire sauce. Season well with salt and ground black pepper.

6 Cover the pan and cook at Gas mark 3, 325°F, 160°C for 2 hours until the meat is tender. Cool and spoon into a deep 2½pt (1.25 litre) pie dish. If you have time, cover and chill overnight, so that the flavours have time to develop. Reserve any remaining sauce to serve with the finished pie.

8 Press the edges of the pastry together well and trim. Knock up pastry by marking horizontal indentations in the pastry edge with the back of a knife. Flute by pressing two fingers on to the edge of the pastry and making a small cut between the fingers evenly round edge.

9 Mark veins on leaves cut from trimmings. Make a rose by cutting a strip ½in (1cm) wide. Cut a scalloped edge and brush with egg. Roll up and place on pie. Brush with egg and cook at Gas mark 7, 425°F, 220°C for 20min, then Gas mark 5, 375°F, 190°C for 20min until well-risen and golden.

MEAT DISHES

Michael Smith's Steak and Kidney Pudding

'All my life, I have been a chauvinist about English cookery, and I use it as a basis for all my food writings, as well as actual cookery. I have fought a battle for English food, not only because I think it is best for us, but because every country, county and region needs an identity. Britain has a national bill of fare and one to be proud of,' writes Michael Smith. If anyone knows about traditional English cookery, this born-and-bred true Yorkshire trencherman certainly does. His reputation and flair, not only for food but also for design, spread to Harewood House, where he masterminded many elaborate banquets in the 1950s ... responsible for handling priceless plate and Derby and Sèvres dinner services, preparing huge silver candelabra for the top tables, festooning fresh flowers for the buffet table and organizing every detail, from food and flowers to security (even the cloakroom attendants were under his command). French food was served then – the only food considered suitable for such an occasion in those days, but, says Michael, 'If I were to plan such a function today, the food I'd choose would be very English. It was

'A good English steak and kidney pudding can be one of the best dishes you will ever serve if you start off with a decent suet pastry'

during this time that I realized that there was, in fact, a culinary history to match the "grace and flavour"' (much later to become the title of his BBC *Pebble Mill at One* cookery series). His interest in English cooking was well under way and the next twenty years were spent delving, reading, experimenting, cooking and eating many of the recipes found in old English recipe books.

Mrs Beeton's cookery book was one of his major references when Michael was asked to be culinary adviser, cook and TV montage creator for the whole series of *Upstairs, Downstairs* and later *The Duchess of Duke Street*. Michael has also conceived and designed three of London's top restaurants, and still finds time to write: 'Steak and kidney pudding is a great favourite of mine. I often serve it for Sunday lunch with creamy, buttery, nutmeg-sprinkled mashed potatoes. Death for those on a diet – so maybe the crust is enough!' And the crust, of course, is a subject that had Michael delving into history again . . .

'Whoever it was who thought up the idea of encasing meat or fruit inside a blanket of flour-and-water paste started the ball rolling for all the pastry cases we know today. But the growth of this type of suet pastry became stunted in Britain, and instead of the quality of the mixture developing and improving, it stayed at the poor end of the scale. Just when these puddings were elevated from cloth to cloth-covered basin remains vague; it was probably in the latter part of the eighteenth century, for by early Victorian times, the basin was in use as a container for puddings, and now that we have "waterproof" foil readily at hand, even the soggy pudding cloth is disappearing.

'Since I never have a "spare" five or six hours to steam a pud, I cook the steak and kidney first, then the whole pudding has a final 1½ hours steaming, making my suet puddings very light-crusted.'

SERVES 6–8
INGREDIENTS:

FOR THE FILLING:
2 lb (1 kg) best stewing steak
8 oz (250 g) ox kidney
8 oz (250 g) button mushrooms
1 onion
flour for dredging
salt and pepper
1 oz (25 g) butter
2 tablespoons oil
½ pt (300 ml) red wine
½ pt (300 ml) beef stock
1 bay leaf
FOR THE PASTRY:
8 oz (250 g) self-raising flour
salt and pepper
1 heaped tablespoon freshly chopped parsley
1 teaspoon grated lemon rind
3 oz (75 g) shredded suet
2 oz (50 g) butter
juice of ½ lemon
1 egg, size 5

Cut 2 lb (1 kg) best stewing steak into 1 in (2.5 cm) cubes. Skin 8 oz (250 g) ox kidney, discard core and cut into cubes. Place 1 heaped tbsp flour and a good shake of salt and pepper into a large polythene bag, add the steak and kidney, a little at a time, and toss in flour until completely covered.

To make the pastry, sift 8 oz (250 g) self-raising flour into a bowl. Add a good shake of salt and a dash of pepper. Now add 1 heaped tbsp freshly chopped parsley and 1 tsp grated lemon rind. Lightly toss in 3 oz (75 g) shredded suet and grate 2 oz (50 g) cold, hard butter into the bowl. Stir with a fork until evenly distributed.

Fill your basin with steak and kidney mixture, making sure the meat is just covered with gravy (the balance of the gravy can be served separately). Roll out the remaining quarter of the pastry to fit the top of the basin. Wet the edges of the pastry and place the lid over, pressing edges well together to seal.

Heat 1 oz (25 g) butter and 2 tbsp oil in a large, heavy-bottomed frying pan until smoking. Fry the sliced onion until golden brown, removing it with a draining spoon to an ovenproof casserole. Add the floured meats to the frying pan and fry until brown on all sides, adding more oil and butter if needed.

Add the quartered mushrooms to the casserole, shake over any remaining flour from the bag and mix in well. Pour over ½ pt (300 ml) red wine, ½ pt (300 ml) beef stock, and add 1 bay leaf. Cover with a lid, and place in a preheated moderate oven (Gas mark 4, 350°F, 180°C). Cook for 1½ hours.

Make a well in the centre. Squeeze the juice of half a lemon into a measuring jug, and make up to a scant 6 fl oz (175 ml) with cold water. Stir the egg, water and lemon juice into the dry ingredients and gather into a soft paste with the fork. Turn on to a floured surface and knead lightly into a soft, loose dough.

Thickly butter a 3 pt (1.5 litre) china pudding basin. Cut off a generous quarter of the dough for the lid. Roll out the rest into a large circle and line the basin. The pastry is soft enough to knuckle into shape. Make sure it comes right to the top of the basin and is an even thickness all round.

Cut out an oval of foil, butter well, then make a pleat across the top; there must be plenty of room to allow the crust to rise, or it will be a soggy mass. Cover and tie firmly with string, looping and tying it loosely two or three times over the top to make a handle for removing the pud from its steaming hot pan.

If you employ the pan method of steaming, let the water come at least two thirds of the way up the basin and keep gently boiling, topping up when necessary. If you use a steamer, the water should boil at a steady rate and will need constant topping up. Steam for 1½ hours.

Claudia Roden's Moussaka

Claudia Roden's unquenchable thirst for new recipes has led her all over the Middle East, including her homeland Egypt. 'My pockets are always full of cooking instructions I've obtained at a chance meeting and my kitchen drawers are full of recipes written in different hands.'

'When I started researching back in the 1960s, people wondered if I would find recipes for sheep's eyes and testicles!' Claudia's work has helped to dismiss such myths. 'Now,' she says, 'there's a new readiness to try unusual combinations of ingredients. And these days, with the proliferation of Middle Eastern restaurants, we have these dishes on our streets, while in supermarkets traditional ingredients – bulgar wheat and pitta bread – disappear quickly from the shelves.

'Moussaka readily comes to my mind as the epitome of Middle Eastern food – beautifully mellow layers of soft aubergine and cinnamon-spiced lamb, topped with a gently set egg sauce with a hint of nutmeg. What could be more perfect served simply with a dish of sweet tomatoes and olives, and eaten in the company of good friends?

'A splendid meal in itself, this dish is a favourite throughout the Middle East'

'Although the Greeks claim moussaka as their own, its name is an Arabic one and it owes much to the influence of the Turkish style of cooking. It is the Turks who regard the aubergine as the king of all vegetables. But don't spoil its unique flavour by taking short cuts. If aubergines are not salted and rinsed first, their otherwise bitter flavour will ruin all your efforts.

'Middle Eastern cooking, though sometimes elaborate, is easy. Some dishes may take time to prepare, but if you consider cooking to be a pleasurable and creative activity, then you are adding the peace and pleasure from its preparation to the enjoyment of serving and eating the dish.

'Cooking in the Middle East is deeply traditional – an inherited art, passed on from mother to daughter. It is not precise and sophisticated, its virtue is loyalty to custom. Yet each cook feels she can improvise within the boundaries of tradition. She can use her artfulness and wits, her sensuous feeling for the food, its texture and aroma to create a new and exquisite dish with the imprint of her own individual taste.

'Timing is not so important, though, and no harm is done if a dish is left to simmer a little longer. Because long, slow cooking is favoured, Middle Eastern food is ideally suited to economical cuts of lamb, either on the bone or minced. It was customary in the past to send large dishes to the local bakery to be cooked. People hurried about the streets with huge casseroles – sometimes balancing them on their heads. Life at the ovens bustled with activity and humour. I'm told of great-aunts who sealed their dishes with a flour and water paste to ensure that no one introduced an unwholesome ingredient out of spite! Today dishes are cooked in domestic ovens, but slowly, as before.

'For an extra-rich moussaka, sprinkle a little grated Kephalotiri or Parmesan cheese over each layer of aubergines. Thinly sliced Gruyère is lovely, too. Sliced courgettes are sometimes used instead of, or with aubergines. A variation popular in Britain makes use of sautéed sliced potatoes instead of the aubergines. Whichever way you choose, moussaka is a splendid meal in itself.'

SERVES 6
INGREDIENTS:

3 aubergines
salt and ground black pepper
oil for frying
2 large onions
1 large tomato (about 8 oz/250 g)
small bunch parsley, chopped (about 3 tablespoons)
1½ lb (750 g) minced lamb or beef
1 teaspoon ground cinnamon or ½ teaspoon ground allspice
2 tablespoons tomato purée
FOR THE WHITE SAUCE:
1 pt (600 ml) milk
2 oz (50 g) butter
2 oz (50 g) plain flour
2 eggs
pinch grated nutmeg

1 Trim off stalk and pointed tip of 3 aubergines and discard. Slice thinly and layer in a colander, sprinkling each layer generously with salt. Leave for at least 30 min for the bitter juices to drain away.

4 Thinly slice 2 large onions. Skin 1 large tomato and chop. Finely chop a small bunch of parsley.

7 Lightly beat 2 eggs in a small bowl. Slowly pour in a little of the hot sauce, whisking with a fork. Pour back into the pan slowly, stirring constantly. Season to taste with salt and ground black pepper and a pinch of grated nutmeg.

2 Wash aubergine slices in cold water and rinse away salt and remaining juices. Squeeze dry with the fingertips and place on kitchen paper.

3 Heat a little oil in a large frying pan and fry a few aubergine slices at a time. Press slices flat and fry quickly until lightly browned, turning once. Drain and place on kitchen paper. Repeat with remaining aubergine.

5 Fry sliced onion in 2 tbsp oil until pale golden. Add minced lamb or beef and fry until well browned. Season and flavour with 1 tsp ground cinnamon or ½ tsp ground allspice. Add 2 tbsp tomato purée and the chopped tomato and parsley. Stir well, moisten with a few tablespoons of water and simmer for 15 min.

6 Prepare a white sauce by heating 1 pt (600 ml) milk in a saucepan until almost boiling. Pour into a jug and rinse pan. Melt 2 oz (50 g) butter in the saucepan. Stir in 2 oz (50 g) plain flour and cook over a low heat for a few min until well blended. Add the hot milk gradually, stirring until it boils.

8 Spoon alternate layers of aubergine and the meat mixture into a deep 4 pt (2 litre) ovenproof dish, starting and finishing with a layer of aubergine.

9 Pour sauce over the aubergine and bake, uncovered, at Gas mark 4, 350°F, 180°C for 45 min to 1 hour until a brown crust has formed on the top and the layers have fused and blended. Serve hot, straight from the dish.

The Wellington Club's Beef Wellington

Who better to ask for a very special Beef Wellington recipe than the Wellington Club, one of London's oldest and most exclusive dining clubs, where they specialize in traditional English cooking? The dining room is traditional, too, with sumptuous red decor, original paintings and antique furniture, all helping to recreate an Edwardian ambiance. There is even a romantic curtained alcove for two (in honour of Edward VII's amorous inclinations, staff have nicknamed it 'The Royal Box'!).

To create their speciality, head lunchtime chef Hans Taranowski and head evening chef Patrice Cauchard use only the best ingredients. 'It's a splendid dish; if you cooked it at home, it would be perfect for special occasions, or in place of the turkey at Christmas. Fillet of beef is not cheap but because there's no waste it's really quite good value.'

The Wellington Club flavours the beef with *duxelles* – a mixture of minced mushrooms and sautéed onions, much used in French cooking, and pâté. 'The secret,' says Patrice, 'is to drive off the moisture in the mushrooms or

'We're very proud of our melt-in-the-mouth beef in its gleaming crust'

the *duxelles* will be too wet. Also stir in only a small amount of pâté as the flavour is quite strong and you don't want to overpower the beef.' Hans often adds chopped thyme.

Both chefs were trained to produce their Beef Wellington – or *Bœuf en Croûte* – when working abroad. 'In Switzerland,' says Hans, 'I would cover the beef with a fine slice of pork-back fat'; 'While in Paris,' comments Patrice, 'they preferred a yeast-based brioche pastry.' Their Wellington Club recipe, traditional to British tastes, uses a puff pastry that creates the delicious combination of crisp outer wrapping with lots of buttery layers.

'It's very good tempered,' says Hans, 'and can be made early in the day, wrapped in the pastry and chilled until guests arrive.' Patrice adds, 'You can also prepare the sauce in the morning, but cover it closely with wet grease proof paper or cling film so that a skin doesn't form.'

There is always a large stockpot on the go in the Club kitchen, so they can make up huge quantities of *demi-glace* – a rich brown sauce which is the basis of many French dishes. To turn it into Périgourdine sauce you should, strictly speaking, add truffles; but their price is so astronomically high that the chefs admit they are not for everyday consumption! Patrice adds Madeira to his sauce while Hans prefers sherry and finely chopped black olives because 'the appearance and flavour is very similar to truffles'. Both variations complement the wonderful flavour of the beef.

'Serve Beef Wellington on a large plate to give you room to carve it,' recommends Hans. 'Cut it into thick slices – it's so tender that it's easy to eat.'

'The *duxelles* add an extra element,' enthuses Patrice, 'moist and very tasty, giving a richness to the rare juicy beef and brittle, puff pastry.' And both chefs agree, 'Beef Wellington is a pleasure to cook and a great pleasure to eat – *bon appétit!*'

SERVES 6–8
INGREDIENTS:

2 lb (1 kg) piece of fillet of beef
1 oz (25 g) butter
8 oz (250 g) button mushrooms
1 small onion or 4 oz (125 g) shallots
2 oz (50 g) smooth liver pâté
2 tablespoons fresh white breadcrumbs
1 sprig thyme
salt and freshly ground black pepper
1½ lb (750 g) chilled puff pastry
1 egg yolk, to glaze
fresh thyme, to garnish

FOR THE PÉRIGOURDINE SAUCE:

1 oz (25 g) butter
1 oz (25 g) plain flour
¾ pt (450 ml) good beef stock
2 teaspoons tomato purée
4 tablespoons Madeira or sherry
12 black olives (optional)

Trim fat from a 2 lb (1 kg) fillet of beef. Heat 1 oz (25 g) butter and fry beef for 2 min on each side until evenly browned, pressing with a spatula so it keeps a good shape. Transfer to a roasting tin and cook at Gas mark 7, 425°F, 220°C for 5 min. For medium beef, cook 12 min; for well-done, 20 min. Cool.

Stir in 2 tbsp fresh white breadcrumbs, and 1 finely chopped sprig of thyme, so the mixture is soft, but not dry. Season with salt and freshly ground black pepper.

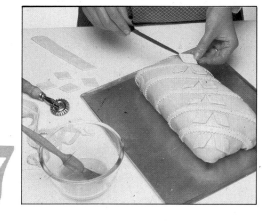

Brush the pastry with egg yolk and decorate. Cut long strips with a pastry wheel and arrange in wide diagonal bars with leaves in between (alternatively, cut tiny stars with a small cutter). Brush decorations with egg yolk. Cook at Gas mark 6, 400°F, 200°C for 40 min until golden brown. Cover with foil if it over-browns.

2 Process or coarsely mince 8 oz (250 g) button mushrooms and 1 small onion or 4 oz (125 g) shallots to make the *duxelles*.

3 Fry the *duxelles* in the meat juices for 5 min until the onion is softened and the moisture from the mushrooms is driven off. Stir in 2 oz (50 g) smooth liver pâté. Cool.

5 Roll out 1½ lb (750 g) chilled puff pastry on a lightly floured surface. Trim to a rectangle 16 × 18 in (40 × 45 cm). Spoon a little *duxelles* down the centre of the pastry and place the fillet of beef on top. Spoon remaining *duxelles* over the top and sides of the beef.

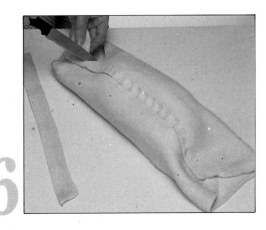

6 Brush the edges of the pastry with beaten egg yolk and fold the pastry over to enclose the beef. Press the edges together to seal well. Trim the excess pastry from the ends and fold over like a parcel. Place the Beef Wellington, join side underneath, on a lightly greased baking sheet.

8 For the Périgourdine Sauce, heat 1 oz (25 g) butter in a saucepan. Stir in 1 oz (25 g) plain flour and mix to a smooth paste with a wooden spoon. Cook for about 5 min, until golden brown. This gives the sauce its colour.

9 Gradually stir in ¾ pt (450 ml) good beef stock, 2 tsp tomato purée and 4 tbsp Madeira or sherry. Bring to the boil, stirring until smooth and glossy. Season with salt and ground black pepper. Add 12 finely chopped black olives, if liked. Serve beef on a large dish, garnished with fresh thyme. Serve the sauce separately.

Lourdes Nichols's Chile con Carne

Lourdes Nichols has probably done more than anyone to introduce Mexican cuisine to Britain. Born and brought up in Mexico City, Lourdes (pronounced Lordeth) came to live in Britain when she married a Yorkshireman. Naturally, she couldn't leave behind her love of her native cuisine and the spicy recipes her mother taught her. 'The sort of 'chilli' most people in this country know is an American interpretation of Mexican food. I make Chile con Carne *my* way – the Mexican way!

'In Mexico,' says Lourdes, 'mealtimes are happy times. We say that the best sauce to a meal is loving preparation with some laughter for good measure. Mexicans are known for their hospitality – entertaining is casual and takes place very often.'

Soon, Lourdes's new friends were asking for lessons in Mexican cookery – how to make tortillas, prepare chillies or bean dishes. 'Many of the ingredients we all use regularly originated in the Americas – chocolate, vanilla, peanuts, avocados, potatoes, beans, corn and turkey – and they all feature in Mexican cooking.' All these, as well as a

'To Mexicans, the best sauce to a meal is loving preparation with some laughter for good measure'

wide variety of beans, fresh herbs, spices and exotic vegetables, are readily available.

Since those early cookery lessons, Lourdes has built up a thriving catering business. 'Mexican food is becoming extremely popular in Britain,' says Lourdes. She is kept busy organizing such events as 'Mexican week' in Kingston, Jamaica, where she found herself cooking and serving 1,000 meals in one week!

As well as her daunting workload, Lourdes also looks after her husband, three teenage children and her elderly mother, who lives with the family in Buckinghamshire.

'Perhaps Mexican food owes some of its new popularity to the fact that it's economical and healthy. Meat is very expensive so recipes are not based around it as they are in Europe. Mexican meat is lean, but always used sparingly. Beans, tortillas and garnishes stretch even the smallest amount. My Chile con Carne is a good example. It gets its spicy flavour from a careful blend of 13 spices and herbs. It's a main course dish and this quantity serves ten to 12 people. You can, of course, make a half quantity but it freezes and reheats so well that it's a good idea to do the whole batch.

'To complete your informal Mexican meal, add a few authentic touches: background music and the essential tequila – our famous spirit made from the agave plant and distilled in Mexico. Now you're all set, so – as we say there – *Buen provecho amigos*, or "Good appetite, friends!"'

SERVES 10–12
INGREDIENTS:

1 lb (500 g) dried red kidney beans
2 lb (1 kg) stewing steak (or pork)
sugar
salt
½ teaspoon black pepper
2 tablespoons malt vinegar
4 large cloves garlic
8 tablespoons oil
2 bay leaves
2 large onions
2 tablespoons mild chilli powder
6 sprigs fresh coriander
½ teaspoon dried oregano
½ teaspoon dried marjoram
½ teaspoon dried thyme
¼ teaspoon ground cumin
12 cloves
2 in (5 cm) cinnamon stick
1 tablespoon cayenne
1 teaspoon sesame seeds
2 × 14 oz (397 g) cans tomatoes
2 chicken stock cubes
5 oz (150 g) tomato purée
2 green chillies

Place 1 lb (500 g) red kidney beans carefully in a large bowl. Cover the beans with cold water and wash them, changing the water several times until it is clear. Drain, then cover the beans with enough cold water to come about 6 in (15 cm) above them. Leave the beans to soak overnight.

Heat 6 tbsp oil in a large casserole. Add the meat and fry until it is golden brown all over. Drain off oil and reserve it. Add 2 bay leaves and 1¼ pt (750 ml) water. Cover and simmer for about 1 hour or until tender. Discard bay leaves. Drain off stock, put ¼ pt (150 ml) in a blender, reserve rest.

Tip two 14 oz (397 g) cans tomatoes and juice into a bowl and mash well. Add to fried paste with 2 chicken stock cubes, and 5 oz (150 g) tomato purée. Mix well, then stir in stock reserved from meat. Simmer for 20 min, stirring occasionally.

2 Cut 2 lb (1 kg) lean stewing steak (or pork) into 1½ in (4 cm) cubes. Put into a large bowl and add ¼ tsp sugar, ¾ tsp salt, ½ tsp freshly ground black pepper and 2 tbsp malt vinegar. Mix well, cover and marinate overnight in the refrigerator.

3 Next day, tip the beans into a large pan and top up with more water. Add 2 large garlic cloves, on a wooden cocktail stick for easy removal. Bring to boil; cook at a rolling boil for the first 15 min to neutralize toxins in beans. Continue cooking for up to 3 hours or until very soft. Top up with boiling water frequently.

5 Chop 1 large onion, add to blender with 2 tbsp chilli powder; blend to a paste. Add 2 garlic cloves, 6 sprigs fresh coriander, ½ tsp each dried oregano, marjoram and thyme, ¼ tsp ground cumin, 12 cloves, 2 in (5 cm) cinnamon stick, 1 tbsp cayenne and 1 tsp sesame seeds. Blend until smooth.

6 Remove the meat from the casserole. Heat up reserved oil in it. Add the spicy paste and fry for about 4 min, stirring continually, until it dries a little. Take care as the mixture tends to splutter.

8 Discard garlic from beans. Add 2 tsp salt and 2 tsp sugar, cook for 10 min. Meanwhile, heat 2 tbsp oil in a frying pan, and fry 1 chopped onion until golden. Add the oil, onion and 2 green chillies to the beans. Simmer for 15 min or until liquid thickens. To hasten this, mash a few beans against the side of the pan.

9 Discard the chillies. Add the beans in their thickened liquid to the spicy sauce and simmer for 15 min. Stir in the meat and bring back to the boil. Simmer very gently for further 30 min. Serve Chile con Carne with rice, a mixed salad, a side dish of finely chopped raw onion, and fresh, warm tortillas or French bread.

Valentina Harris's Lasagne al Forno

To Valentina Harris fresh pasta is the most natural thing in the world. Born and brought up in Italy, pasta has been part of her life, eaten at every other meal, 'if not every meal!' she exclaims. 'To me, it's not new or different, but in this country it is just beginning to come into its own. Everyone has realized that pasta is nutritious, cheap, delicious *and* versatile. It's not just in Italy that new recipes and ways of eating and serving pasta are invented. Without a doubt it is now generally accepted that with pasta, anything goes, although I prefer to eat it in the traditional way. But mine is a highly personal opinion. There are many new recipes for pasta which contain unusual ingredients, are quick to prepare and taste delicious.

'Basically, when it comes to cooking and serving pasta, you must do as your spirit takes you. There are just two standard rules I must insist upon: firstly, unless it is a cold dish, pasta must be served as piping hot as possible, which all depends on speed in draining, dressing and serving it, and secondly, it must *not* be overcooked.'

Valentina came to England seven years ago, to work in

'My favourite stand-by for all occasions – it's a superb meal with a minimum of fuss'

London. She met and married Bob Harris, a broadcaster and journalist, and consequently stayed in Britain. Most of her time now is spent looking after their young son Benjamin, but she also writes books about food and children's short stories. Valentina has studied regional Italian cooking for a book based on the influences of historic events on the local cuisine.

'Baked pasta seems to be popular with almost everyone and is my favourite main dish stand-by for all occasions. For supper parties amongst friends, when you are not going all out to impress anyone, simple dishes provide a perfect solution. You can make everything in advance – all you need to remember is to pop the dish into the oven. Serve it with a salad followed by a simple dessert and there you have it: a superb meal created with a minimum of fuss.

'Pasta dishes can be easily frozen and to do so I suggest you follow the method I have used for years. Instead of buttering the ovenproof dish, line it with freezer clingfilm, then layer the lasagne as usual. Fill the dish to 2 inches from the top to allow for expansion, wrap the clingfilm over the top and freeze. Do not bake before freezing. When frozen, remove the parcel of pasta from the dish and store as normal. When you want to use it, dip the parcel into a basin of very hot water, peel off the cling film and return the pasta to its original dish, this time buttered. Thaw and bake as usual, or place frozen in a cool oven until heated through, then raise the heat to brown the top.'

SERVES 6
INGREDIENTS:

PASTA:
14 oz (425 g) strong plain flour
4 fresh eggs
salt
2 tablespoons puréed spinach
2 tablespoons milk or oil
OR 14 oz (425 g) bought fresh green lasagne
MEAT SAUCE:
6 tablespoons olive oil
1 large onion, peeled and chopped
2 carrots, scraped and chopped
2 stalks celery, chopped
1 clove garlic, peeled and chopped
6 oz (175 g) lean minced meat (veal and/or beef)
5 oz (150 g) cooked ham, chopped
6 tablespoons tomato purée diluted in 6 tbsp boiling water
BÉCHAMEL SAUCE:
2¼ oz (60 g) butter
2 oz (50 g) plain flour
1 pt (600 ml) milk
salt and white pepper
pinch of grated nutmeg
4 oz (125 g) Parmesan, Cheddar or Gruyère cheese, grated
3 oz (75 g) butter

Tip 14 oz (425 g) flour on to your work surface and shape it into a mountain. Make a hollow in the centre, then break 4 eggs into this hollow. Add ½ tsp salt, 2 tbsp puréed spinach and 2 tbsp milk or oil. Whisk the eggs with a fork for a minute.

Flour your work surface and the rolling pin. Flatten the dough and roll out into as perfect a circle as possible. Fold it in half and roll it out again. Continue in this way until you have achieved a smooth, fine sheet of pasta, about ¼ in (5 mm) thick.

Cut the pasta into neat rectangles about 3 × 3½ in (7 × 8 cm) with a sharp knife. Allow to dry on a clean cloth for about 5 min then cook, a few at a time.

Make the sauce. Melt butter in a saucepan. Add flour, remove from heat and mix to a smooth paste. Return to heat and pour in milk. Stir quickly off heat until smooth. Season, then simmer gently, stirring, for 15 to 20 min. Add 2 oz (50 g) cheese.

2

Begin to mix together using a circular motion. Start from the centre and work outwards. Use one hand for mixing and the other to hold the mound in place. When all the flour has been absorbed, push and squeeze into a lump of dough.

3

Using both hands, press down with the heel of your palm and begin to pull and knead the dough. Keep turning, kneading and folding until you have a smooth, elastic consistency (about 10 min). Set aside to rest under a tea towel for 5 min.

5

Roll the pasta out as thin as possible; curl the end furthest from you around the rolling pin and push the rolling pin backwards and forwards, pressing firmly to stretch the pasta. Work very quickly or the pasta will dry out and be impossible to work with.

6

When you have rolled and thinned about one half of the pasta, turn it around and roll the other end in the same way to stretch and thin the dough. Repeat this process about eight times, turning the pasta until it is about ⅛ in (3 mm) thick.

8

Bring 7 pt (3.5 litres) of water and 4 tsp salt to fast boil in a large saucepan with a lid. Add lasagne four at a time. Stir well to prevent sticking, cover saucepan and bring back to boil: test after 4 min. When cooked, lay pieces side by side on a wet cloth.

9

Heat 6 tbsp olive oil in a large pan. Add the onion, carrots, celery and garlic. Fry until the onion is transparent. Add the meat and brown gently for about 10 min. Add cooked ham and diluted tomato purée: cook gently for about 30 min then season.

11

Butter a 4 pt (2 litre) shallow ovenproof dish and cover base with ⅓ of lasagne. Spread with about ½ meat and ⅓ béchamel, then cover with another ⅓ of lasagne. Sprinkle cheese and dot butter between meat and lasagne. Repeat, finishing with béchamel.

12

Dot the top with butter and sprinkle over the rest of the grated cheese. Bake in a preheated hot oven (Gas mark 7, 425°F, 220°C) for 20 min, or until top is browned and crispy. Remove from oven and allow to rest about 5 min before serving.

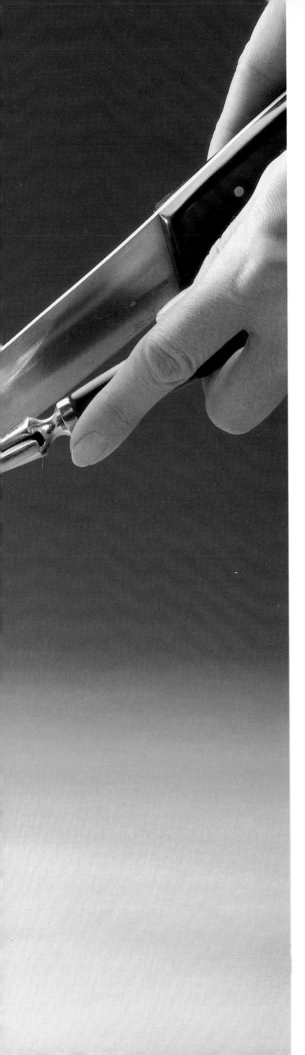

Arabella Boxer's Crown Roast of Lamb

Arabella Boxer believes British cooking can be cultivated and improved immeasurably without making vast efforts. 'Am I the only person who doesn't want to compete with professional chefs?' she asks. 'I find it hard to believe that there aren't thousands of others, like myself, who want to cook in a more relaxed way, for the sheer pleasure of it, and for the fun of eating simple dishes.'

Arabella is certainly a champion of 'real food'. By this she means 'fresh ingredients, cooked for the most part in classic ways. Raw ingredients lie at the root of our cooking and must be treated with respect.'

Meat is the most difficult food to buy well, because its good qualities, or lack of them are not in the main discernible to the eye. The way meat looks is, of course, important and provides valuable pointers, but it isn't the whole story. A lot depends on the age and breed of the animal, how it was reared, at what temperature it was slaughtered and, most important of all, how long it was hung afterwards.

Young lamb should be firm and pinkish, the bones

'British lamb, without a doubt, is the most tender and has the best flavour, and a crown roast is elegant and very English'

should be small with a blue tinge, and the fat creamy white and crisp. The more mature the lamb, the redder its flesh and the more richly coloured its fat.

Arabella likes to concentrate on techniques just as much as ingredients. Her writing includes explanations of methods with background information and tips. 'Roasting,' she says, 'is one of the few kitchen processes which has suffered, rather than gained, from modern technology. In the past, huge joints of meat were roasted on a horizontal spit over an open fire. In the nineteenth century, as wood fires gave way to coal, the fireplace changed its shape and the spit became perpendicular so the meat hung in front of, rather than over the fire. Fat clings to a rotating joint instead of dripping off, ensuring constant self-basting, and also the heat of the fire was reflected by a screen, which probably brought the art of roasting to its height.

'True roasting is like grilling, since the meat cooks by direct exposure to radiant heat rather than being enclosed in hot air, as in the modern oven. Unless we use a rotisserie, which is closer to the old method, we are really subjecting our meat to a combination of baking and steaming.

'But we can still produce good, well cooked dishes if we choose our meat carefully and use our ovens to the best advantage. Only good cuts are suitable for roasting, and on a fairly large scale. The only small joints that are really worth roasting are those that are an entity in themselves, such as a rack of lamb, or a bird.

'People find roasting demanding because timing is crucial, and if they overcook the meat, it could be ruined and the investment in terms of a large piece of meat is great. Unfortunately, most people don't roast meat often enough, so they don't get a chance to practise. However, roasting is so simple that keen cooks can experiment and feel free to add their own variations.

'When entertaining, remember that it isn't just the food that's important – I care more about creating an atmosphere where my friends feel relaxed and at ease than stunning them with elaborate dishes. For a small party, a crown roast of lamb is ideal. It's a very pretty way of presenting meat, simple but elegant, and although the joint is small, it works well with the roasting method.'

INGREDIENTS:

2 racks of lamb (best end)
1 small onion
1 carrot
1 stalk celery
5 black peppercorns
¼pt (150ml) red or white wine or 3 tablespoons red wine vinegar (see step 6)
8oz (250g) fresh or frozen peas
12oz (375g) young carrots
½oz (15g) butter
salt and pepper

Take 2 racks of lamb and have them chined. Place fat side down, and cut and scrape meat away from chine bone (at end of ribs). Remove bone and reserve. Repeat on other rack.

Make shallow cuts along sides of each bone about 1½in (4cm) long – don't cut right through. Slide the knife under each rib bone and cut meat away from bone. Fold flap of meat over to fat side. Scrape meat away from bone tips, leaving them clean. Repeat.

Preheat the oven to hot (Gas mark 7, 425°F, 220°C). Put the roast on a rack in a roasting tin. The roasting rack holds the meat out of the fat while cooking: meat should not roast sitting in a puddle of fat.

Return the meat to the oven and cook for 45 to 50min, basting two or three times more with stock. Meanwhile, cook shelled peas, fresh or frozen, and young carrots, thickly sliced, separately. Drain, then mix, adding butter, and seasoning.

2

With rack still fat side down, make ½ to 1 in (1–2.5 cm) cuts at base of rib bones, between the ribs and partly through the thickest part of the meat. Make cuts just deep enough to allow the rack to be curled into a semicircle. Repeat with other rack.

3

Feel for the small flap of cartilage in one side of the rack. Working from this side, loosen a corner of the thin, papery skin that covers the fat. Tear it away in one piece. It's important to start from the cartilage side or the fat will tear. Cut out cartilage. Repeat.

5

Place the racks fat side together. Hold end bones together, loop trussing needle with string behind bone at rib base, pull through, cut string and knot. Repeat about 1 in (2.5 cm) from top edge of meat. Curve into a crown, then make 2 stitches at other end.

6

Put the meat trimmings in a pressure cooker with onion, carrot, celery, all cut in half. Add a pinch of salt and peppercorns. Add wine and ½ pt (300 ml) cold water *or* red wine vinegar and ¾ pt (450 ml) water. Cook for 30 to 40 min on High pressure.

8

Wrap the tip of each bone in a tiny cap of foil to prevent it burning. Roast joint for 15 min, then reduce heat to moderate (Gas mark 4, 350°F, 180°C) and pour off the fat collected in the roasting tin.

9

Strain stock from pressure cooker. Let it stand for a moment or two to allow the fat to rise to the top; remove the fat from the surface and baste the meat with some of the clear, hot stock.

11

When the meat is cooked, transfer to a serving dish. Allow to rest, uncovered, about 15 min in a warm place. Put the tin over a moderate heat, add any remaining stock and bubble the juices for a couple of minutes.

12

Fill the crown with the peas and carrots. Remove the foil from bone tips and add paper frills if liked. You may need to remove them for carving.

Arto der Haroutunian's Armenian Kebab

'Simple to prepare and simple to digest' – that's a major characteristic of Middle Eastern cuisine, and one that Arto der Haroutunian actively promotes. Arto spent his early childhood in Aleppo, Syria. His father's family originated from Cilicia (southern Turkey) and his mother's from Armenia. Arto grew up in Britain, but was very much influenced by the Middle Eastern customs and traditions kept by his family and friends. Today, he and his brother are the proud owners of a chain of Armenian restaurants in the Manchester area. Arto is convinced that many of our western culinary traditions sprang from the Middle East, a result of thousands of years of experimentation. 'Kebabs began,' he says, 'in the Middle East.

'Before you begin cooking, though, a word of warning: there are too many dishes falsely labelled "kebab". The word simply means "cooked meat" – in the oven or over fire – and is derived from one of the early Indian languages, not Turkish as is often claimed. But the secret of a good kebab lies in the marination – steeping meat in oil and spices – and then cooking over wood or charcoal. *Şiş*

'Any kebab that is not marinated or basted is not a kebab, but merely grilled or barbecued meat'

kebab (pronounced "shish") is by far the most famous Middle Eastern dish and has countless local variations. *Şiş* is the name given to chunks of meat – lamb or goat – threaded on to wooden sticks and grilled over dried wood.

'Lamb has always been the most popular meat in the Middle East. Indeed, to an Arab, "meat" simply means lamb or mutton. All kebabs are traditionally served on a bed of rice (pilav) or bulgar, also called cracked wheat.

'Rice is also part of the staple diet, with Basmati rice the most popular. A dish of plain boiled rice is never served. A light fluffy pilav is the desired end result, with each grain firm and separate and usually with a slight golden hue. In short, it should never have a sticky or mushy consistency. To achieve the perfect end, follow the recipe to the letter, for the amount of liquid used will be crucial in determining the final outcome of the pilav. To serve with kebabs, I add a buttery date and almond topping *(see Step 9)* – rosewater is available from good chemists.

'Middle Eastern food is spicy, but not hot, and subtle use is made of fresh herbs and spices. Tomatoes, herbs and spices make delicious sauces, though more often than not nowadays tomato purée is used instead of tomatoes. Although kebabs are sometimes served "dry" I like to serve them with this typical Armenian sauce – it's a family recipe that we use in our restaurants.'

SERVES 4
INGREDIENTS:

2 lb (1 kg) lamb or beef
1 onion
1 green pepper
4 oz (125 g) small mushrooms
4 small tomatoes
bay leaves
FOR THE MARINADE:
¼ pt (150 ml) green olive oil
1 teaspoon ground allspice
¼ pt (150 ml) red wine
salt and black pepper
FOR THE RICE PILAV:
9 oz (275 g) Basmati rice
4 oz (125 g) butter
2 oz (50 g) blanched almonds
3 oz (75 g) dates
2 oz (50 g) seedless raisins
1 teaspoon rosewater
FOR THE SAUCE:
4 tablespoons oil
1 small onion, peeled and finely chopped
1 clove garlic, peeled and crushed
1 green pepper, seeded and chopped
2 large tomatoes, blanched, seeded and chopped
2 tablespoons tomato purée
½ glass red wine (optional)
2 bay leaves
1 teaspoon ground coriander

1

Leg of lamb, particularly the fillet end, is best for kebabs although you could use beef. Feel around the bone then cut meat away from it. Slice across into 3 thick slices. Trim off the skin and fat, remove tough membranes and ligaments and cut the meat into neat chunks.

4

Thread the meat on to skewers, together with pieces of onion, green pepper, mushrooms, halved tomatoes and bay leaves. Cut onion into quarters, trim away root, then separate the layers. Trim away seeds and white pith from pepper, cut lengthwise into 1 in (2.5 cm) strips, then cut into squares.

7

After the rice has been cooking for 20 min, the grains should be tender and separate and there should be small holes in the surface of the rice. Turn off the heat, remove the lid, cover with a tea towel, replace the lid and leave to 'rest' for 10 to 15 min before spooning on to serving dish.

2

This is my favourite Armenian marinade. I like to use ¼pt (150ml) green olive oil but you can also use a good vegetable oil. Add 1 tsp ground allspice and ¼pt (150ml) red wine. Then I add about 1½tsp salt and ½tsp black pepper. Mix all the ingredients for the marinade in a large bowl.

3

Add the pieces of meat and turn until they are well coated in the marinade. Cover and leave the meat in the fridge for at least 6 to 8 hours or preferably overnight. Some of the marinade is absorbed into the meat.

5

Wash 9oz (275g) Basmati rice thoroughly and drain. Melt 2oz (50g) butter in a saucepan. Add the rice and fry, stirring frequently, for 2 to 3min. Add 1 tbsp salt and 1pt (600ml) boiling water and boil vigorously for 3min. Cover, lower the heat and simmer for about 20min until liquid is absorbed.

6

Heat 4 tbsp oil in a large pan, add onion, garlic, green pepper, and fry until onion is golden. Add tomatoes and tomato purée, 1pt (600ml) water, red wine (optional), bay leaves, coriander, salt and pepper to taste and stir well. Bring to the boil, cook for 15 to 20min, stirring occasionally, until reduced by one third.

8

Meanwhile, cook kebabs over charcoal or under the preheated grill. It's essential that the grill is really hot to sear the outside of the meat and seal in the juices. Baste vegetables, particularly the mushrooms, with marinade. Turn the skewers occasionally so that the meat is cooked evenly. Cook for 12 to 15min.

9

Melt 1oz (25g) butter in a large frying pan. Add blanched almonds and fry until golden. Add another 1oz (25g) butter, stoned and sliced dates and seedless raisins. Fry for a few more minutes, stirring. Remove from heat and stir in 1 tsp rosewater. Scatter over rice, arrange kebabs on top and serve with sauce.

Pat Chapman's Rhogan Gosh

Pat Chapman believes his passionate love of curries is due to family links with the Indian subcontinent stretching back over 200 years.

'I'm quite addicted to spicy food; I think it must be in my blood even though my parents left India to settle in England before I was born. I'm sure I'd get withdrawal symptoms if I didn't eat curry regularly. It's strange, though, that we British talk about "curry" – most Indians have no idea what we mean. The word doesn't exist in any of their 15 or so languages.

'One of the difficulties I found when I first started experimenting with cooking my own curries was that they differed greatly from "professional" ones I'd tried. I took some lessons from a Gujarati friend and that improved my cooking enormously, but something still wasn't quite right. So I decided the only way to capture those elusive flavours and textures was to go into the restaurant kitchens and ask the chefs for their secrets.

'One of the best tips I picked up is the onion purée method. It is the basis for nearly all curries and it gives a

'The mild flavour of this authentic Kashmiri recipe is fantastic – deliciously different in spicing and character from other curries'

dish that special texture and consistency we all strive for. I make it up in large batches and freeze it in yogurt pots so that I can produce a meal in a hurry whenever I want.

'The next step is Bhoona – the traditional process of frying the spices in oil to release their pungency. But it is all too easy to burn them, so I always mix the spices to a paste with water then add them to the onion purée. This ensures the spices are properly blended and it influences the final taste of the dish. Don't be tempted to use too much liquid in curries, otherwise you'll never achieve the right texture. Keep an eye on the food while it is cooking and make sure it doesn't stick. You can always add a little water at a later stage if it looks too dry.

'When I first started cooking curries I was using curry powder, one of the reasons why it was so difficult to get a good flavour. With the arrival of the Asian community in this country, spices became much easier to find.

Pat and his wife Fiona Ross formed The Curry Club in 1982. The club now has over 7,000 members who enjoy regular get-togethers at club nights around the country, as well as cookery demonstrations and courses, a quarterly magazine, even gourmet trips to India!

'Rhogan Gosh is one of the traditional dishes from the time of the Moghul emperors and in ancient days they used alkenet root to colour the meat red. Tomato and paprika make a reddish sauce; add red food colouring if you want the meat red, too! There are many versions; my favourite is based on an authentic Kashmiri recipe. The meat is lamb, which is easy to get hold of here and is used a lot in India because pork and beef are forbidden for religious reasons. The onion purée and yogurt give a smooth texture to the subtly spiced and mildly hot mixture. Fresh green coriander – one of the great additives to curries – gives a delicious taste when added towards the end of cooking or used as a garnish. The dish as a whole is extremely easy to make and has a truly fantastic flavour.'

SERVES 6
INGREDIENTS:

3 green cardamoms
3 cloves
3 small pieces cassia bark
¹/₂ teaspoon turmeric
¹/₂ teaspoon chilli powder
1 teaspoon ground coriander
1 teaspoon ground cumin
1¹/₂ lb (750 g) lean lamb
4 fl oz (125 ml) natural yogurt
salt
8 oz (250 g) onions
2 in (5 cm) fresh root ginger
2 cloves garlic
1 × 14 oz (397 g) can or 14 oz (425 g) fresh tomatoes
5 tablespoons ghee or oil
2 teaspoons garam masala
2 teaspoons paprika
1 tablespoon chopped fresh coriander

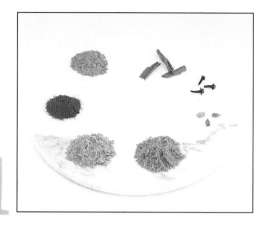

Assemble the following spices, from top: 3 green cardamoms, 3 cloves, 3 small pieces cassia bark, ½ tsp turmeric, ½ tsp chilli powder, 1 tsp ground coriander, 1 tsp ground cumin. Cassia bark is a corky bark with a sweet fragrance, similar to cinnamon, but coarser – you could substitute a cinnamon stick if necessary.

For the onion purée, peel and roughly chop 8 oz (250 g) onions and a 2 in (5 cm) piece of fresh root ginger. Peel 2 cloves garlic. Prepare 14 oz (400 g) tomatoes, canned or fresh.

Put the lamb and yogurt mixture into another saucepan. Cook over a low heat for 25 min, stirring occasionally to prevent sticking. Add a little salt to taste.

Trim 1½lb (750 g) lean lamb and cut into cubes. Choose leg for leanness; shoulder is cheaper but needs more trimming.

Mix together the lamb, spices, 4 fl oz (125 ml) natural yogurt and some salt. Allow this mixture to marinate for a minimum of 6 hours, or preferably overnight.

Put onion, ginger, garlic and tomatoes into a blender and purée until smooth. (This mixture can be prepared in quantity, puréed and frozen for later use.)

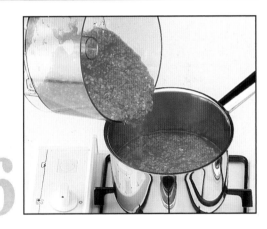

Heat 5 tbsp ghee or oil in a saucepan, and add the onion purée. Cook for 20 min, stirring occasionally. Add salt to taste, about 1 tsp. Ghee (pronounced with a hard g, as in geese) is clarified butter or margarine – it doesn't burn as easily as butter and it adds a wonderful flavour to the curry.

Combine the contents of the two saucepans and cook gently for a further 30 min or so, until the meat is quite tender. If at any time the curry gets too dry, add a little water.

Stir in 2 tsp garam masala, 2 tsp paprika, and 1 tbsp chopped fresh coriander. Mix well and cook for a further 5 min. Put into a serving dish and serve with pilau rice, poppadoms and finely sliced onions.

Michael Smith's Lancashire Hot Pot

'What can beat the simplicity of a large, steaming Lancashire hot pot?' asks Michael Smith, and answers his own question. 'Nothing – it's perfect family fare.' The well-known television cook and writer is passionately enthusiastic about English food. 'Not only because I think it's best for us but because every country and region needs the safety of its own identity. And for me, a hot pot is steaming layers of pure nostalgia instantly bringing back memories of my North Country childhood.

'I grew up in a Yorkshire mill town during the war – where Wednesday was always hot pot day. You could tell which day it was up there just from the smell! The hot pot was still cooked in a fire-oven in a great big tin, 16 by 12 in, and all of us children (I'm the youngest of seven) would fight for the burnt, crispy potatoes from the top. It's essential that the potatoes are crisp on a hot pot – which is the reason I brush them with butter, and it also turns them a marvellous golden colour which is so inviting.

'At home, the hot pot was made with extra gravy which would be spooned over the Yorkshire pudding served with

'Steaming layers of pure nostalgia instantly bring back memories of my North Country childhood'

it. In fact, Yorkshire pud came with every meal – all ten 7-inch, carbohydrate-filled tins of it. The whole meal was cooked together in the fire-oven. The skill of the women in gauging the temperature of the ovens was amazing. Hot pot and pudding would be deftly flicked from one part to the other to get the right heat. It was also traditional to put currants in the pudding on hot pot day to complement the lamb.

'I still like to douse my hot pot with Yorkshire relish (a tangy brown sauce), which sounds terrible but tastes absolutely delicious – pickled red cabbage goes well with it, too. And of course you must mop up your gravy with bread at the end of the meal; I can remember my grandfather picking up his plate and drinking it off!

'Today I'll cook one if all my family is coming round. Ideally it should be part of a big family meal as the beauty of it is the sheer size. And it's a good dish if you're entertaining because it takes a minimum amount of handling – you can put it in the oven and forget about it.

'Of course, with today's small families and the convenience of freezing dishes, it's also sensible to make it in individual ovenproof pots. The method is the same but divide the contents between six ⅔pt (380ml) dishes, and cut 30min off the final cooking time.

'Because we now know it's healthier to cut down on fat wherever possible, I have replaced the traditional neck of lamb with lamb fillet. But what you mustn't tamper with is the potato top. I've also added some dry white wine to it. I did wonder if this was taking a severe liberty; but I think the result proves otherwise. After all, the fact that good English food is starting to be cooked and served with pride again is because French cooking, especially *nouvelle cuisine* gave us a jolt. With a little adaptation, our national dishes can be every bit as delicious.

'Shepherd's Pie, Fish Pie, Lancashire Hot Pot – that's English family cooking at its best. Good, robust, everyone-round-the-table food.'

SERVES 6
INGREDIENTS:

2 lamb fillets, each weighing about 1 lb (500 g)
24 baby onions
3 stalks celery
2 tablespoons olive or soya oil
18 button mushrooms
1 oz (25 g) pearl barley
¼ pt (150 ml) dry white wine
¾ pt (450 ml) chicken stock
salt and freshly ground black pepper
6 potatoes, each weighing 4 oz (125 g)
1 oz (25 g) butter

1 Place 2 lamb fillets on a large chopping board. Discard any fat and cut each fillet into 12 slices.

4 Brown onions over a fairly fierce heat. Add a splash more oil if necessary. Place in casserole dish. Quickly fry chopped celery, 18 button mushrooms and 1 oz (25 g) pearl barley.

7 Peel and finely slice six 4-oz (125-g) potatoes. Arrange overlapping in circles on top of the meat.

112

2 Trim and peel 24 baby onions, leaving them whole. Finely dice 3 trimmed stalks of celery.

3 Heat 2 tbsp olive or soya oil in a frying pan. Quickly fry lamb in small batches to seal and brown meat. Drain well, place in the base of a deep 4 pt (2 litre) casserole dish.

5 Pour off any excess oil and spoon the celery, mushrooms and pearl barley into the casserole dish.

6 Pour over ¼ pt (150 ml) dry white wine mixed with ¾ pt (450 ml) chicken stock to cover the meat. Season lightly with salt and several twists of freshly ground black pepper.

8 Gently heat 1 oz (25 g) butter and brush over the potatoes. Season lightly with salt and freshly ground black pepper. Cover with a lid or foil and cook in a preheated oven, Gas mark 3, 325°F, 160°C for 1½ hours.

9 Remove the lid or foil, raise the temperature to Gas mark 5, 375°F, 190°C, and cook the hot pot for a further 50 to 60 min, or until the potatoes are golden brown.

Ken Hom's Sweet and Sour Pork

The smiling face of Ken Hom became familiar with his television series *Chinese Cooking*, which explained many of the techniques of Chinese cooking, teaching us stir-frying and steaming, uncovering the mystique of such strange-sounding ingredients as hoi-sin sauce, five-spice powder, wuntun skins and glutinous rice, and bringing together all the fascinating foods and flavours that we've tasted in Chinese restaurants.

Ken Hom was born in the USA of Cantonese parents. His culinary training took place in his uncle's restaurant in Chicago where he started to work part-time at the age of 11. In those early days, he had all the routine jobs. 'I remember peeling hundreds of pounds of prawns, a tedious and painful chore.

'Good food has been an important part of my life since my earliest childhood. I well remember my family gathered round, endlessly discussing what we were to eat, how it would be prepared, what our favourite dishes were, and the best methods for cooking various delicacies. In fact, this is a common experience for most Chinese – food is our

'Sweet and sour pork is one of the best known Chinese dishes in the West. It should be so delicately balanced that one is hard-pressed to describe it as strictly sweet or sour'

favourite topic of conversation. For us, food is more than a passion, it is an obsession. The Chinese have an expression: *"Chi fan le mei you?"*, which literally means: "Have you eaten yet?" It is used universally as a greeting, just as one would ask in English, "How are you?" It's also a wish for one's health and happiness.

'All the time I was thus employed I was surrounded by the wonderful aromas of mouthwatering dishes being prepared by expert chefs. Slowly, they taught me why a particular spice went with a certain meat, why this sauce suited that vegetable – in short, the essence of Chinese cooking technique.

'Of all Chinese dishes, Sweet and Sour Pork is probably one of the best known in the West. Unfortunately for Westerners, it is rarely properly made, often consisting of heavy, doughy balls containing a scrap of pork, drenched in a hideously sweet, red sauce. Properly prepared, sweet and sour Chinese dishes are so delicately balanced that one is hard-pressed to describe them as either strictly sweet or sour. In my version of this classic dish you will find that balance.

'There is an old Chinese proverb which says, "To the ruler, people are heaven; to the people, food is heaven." Once you have embarked on the exciting road to discovering the mysteries and pleasures of Chinese cooking, you will soon find how sublime Chinese food can be. I wish you happy cooking and happy eating.'

SERVES 4
INGREDIENTS:

12 oz (375 g) lean pork
1 tablespoon dry pale sherry or rice wine
1 tablespoon light soy sauce
1 teaspoon salt
1 egg, beaten
2 tablespoons cornflour
³⁄₄ pt (450 ml) oil, preferably groundnut
3 oz (75 g) canned lychees, drained, or fresh orange segments
FOR THE SAUCE:
¹⁄₄ pt (150 ml) chicken stock
1 tablespoon light soy sauce
¹⁄₂ teaspoon salt
1¹⁄₂ tablespoons cider vinegar or Chinese white rice vinegar
1 tablespoon sugar
1 tablespoon tomato purée
¹⁄₂ green pepper
¹⁄₂ red pepper
2 oz (50 g) carrots
2 oz (50 g) spring onions
1 teaspoon cornflour
spring onions, to garnish

Cut 12 oz (375 g) lean pork into 1 in (2.5 cm) cubes. Most Chinese think of 'meat' as being pork. An extremely versatile meat, it can be prepared in many different ways. You should use tender pork steaks (from leg) or pork fillet for deep-frying.

Make batter by mixing 1 egg and 2 tbsp cornflour in a bowl until well blended. This batter protects food during deep-frying by helping to seal in juices. Lift pork cubes out of marinade, put them into batter and coat well.

Remove pork pieces from batter. Make sure excess batter drips off before adding the pieces to hot oil with slotted spoon. Deep-fry them until batter is crisp and golden. Drain deep-fried pork cubes on kitchen paper. Keep warm.

2 Put pork cubes in bowl together with 1 tbsp dry pale sherry or rice wine, 1 tbsp light soy sauce and 1 tsp salt. Marinate for 20 min to infuse flavour and tenderize meat. Light soy sauce – essential to Chinese cooking – is made from a mixture of soya beans, flour and water fermented and distilled.

3 Meanwhile, cut half a green pepper and half a red pepper into 1 in (2.5 cm) squares. Peel and cut 2 oz (50 g) carrots and 2 oz (50 g) spring onions into 1 in (2.5 cm) pieces. The uniform size of meat and vegetables adds to the visual appeal of the dish. Blanch carrots in boiling water for 4 min. Drain and set aside.

5 Heat ¾ pt (450 ml) oil in a large wok until almost smoking. You may find a deep-fat fryer safer and easier to use, in which case you will need to use about double the amount of oil, but never fill it more than one third with oil.

6 The trick in deep-fat frying is to regulate the heat so that food is sealed but does not brown so fast that it's uncooked inside. Wait for the oil to get hot enough before adding food. The oil should give off a 'haze' when it is right. Test by dropping in a small piece of food; if it bubbles all over, the oil is hot enough.

8 To make sweet and sour sauce, combine ¼ pt (150 ml) chicken stock with 1 tbsp light soy sauce, ½ tsp salt (omit, if using stock cubes), 1½ tbsp cider vinegar or white rice vinegar, 1 tbsp sugar and 1 tbsp tomato purée, in large saucepan. Bring to the boil and add peppers, carrots and spring onions, stir well.

9 In small bowl, blend together 1 tsp each of cornflour and water. This will thicken sauce and make it velvety. Stir this mixture into sauce and return to boil. Lower heat to a simmer. Add 3 oz (75 g) canned lychees, drained (or use fresh orange segments), and pork cubes. Mix well and reheat. Serve with plain, steamed rice.

Josceline Dimbleby's Cold Spiced Ham

'I can vividly remember the smells and tastes of my travelling childhood,' says Josceline Dimbleby. 'My parents were in the diplomatic service, and I'm sure that those early years we spent travelling in the Middle East and South America developed my passion for herbs, spices and strong, unusual flavours which I use in a lot of my cooking.' Certainly Josceline knows her spices and uses them adventurously in her recipes. She has a way of creating highly original dishes, using simple ingredients, with delicious results.

'Cold Spiced Ham is a mouthwatering way of cooking smoked rolled collar,' says Josceline. 'It's quite cheap to make and so it's perfect for whenever you have to feed a lot of people. It's a very useful joint to have in the summer, particularly the holidays when our children are home from school. We always have cold lunches in the summer – usually salads, sometimes sandwiches or picnics – and this is the perfect thing to have ready and waiting in the fridge when you don't want to have to think about preparing anything! It's absolutely ideal to serve cold, it has a

'With its mellow, aromatic flavour, this is the perfect cut for summer picnics and salad lunches'

wonderfully mellow, aromatic flavour and you can carve it in very thin slices.

'I first tasted a cold spiced ham when I stayed with some friends in Norfolk. I came home all inspired and decided to do a version for myself. Black treacle makes the ham really dark outside; I like its intense flavour – very strong, but not particularly sweet. Muscovado sugar is also suitable, and honey is traditional, but they're both sweeter and not so delicious. You could use a more expensive joint such as gammon. Sometimes, if the collar has a very hard skin I take it off before I cook it, and press the spices on to the layer of fat underneath but, generally, you can cook it with the skin on and remove after baking. If you haven't got time to stick cloves all over the joint, then you can crush them with the allspice if you prefer. I've also had a play with this recipe using only Indian spices – cardamom (don't pod them, just put the whole pods into the grinder), cloves, a stick of cinnamon, and coriander seeds; whizz them all up in the grinder and smear on to the outside of the collar. Sometimes I forget to clean out the grinder after I've crushed a load of spices, but luckily my husband [broadcaster David Dimbleby] likes a lingering spicy flavour in his coffee! It doesn't work the other way round, though; you have to remember to clean away ground coffee before putting any spices in the grinder!

'David has an adventurous taste in food, and I'm sure I would never have become such an enthusiastic cook if it had not been for his constant pleasure and interest in everything I try out. I don't make the food we eat more bland for the children because I think it is important to develop and influence their taste buds from the very start. I get great pleasure from cooking if I can choose a time when there is no need to rush, when there are no distracting children around, pulling at me, asking questions and always wanting to try everything. Just a quiet, clean sunny kitchen and a colourful array of enticing ingredients.'

SERVES 15
INGREDIENTS:

4–5 lb (2–2.25 kg) piece rolled smoked collar
1–2 tablespoons juniper berries
about 1 tablespoon whole cloves
1–2 tablespoons whole allspice berries
1 lb (500 g) black treacle
demerara sugar

Soak a 4–5 lb (2–2.25 kg) piece of rolled smoked collar in cold water for at least 12 hours, changing the water 2 or 3 times. Whatever size you choose, it will shrink a bit in the cooking, but this piece should feed at least 15 people. It will keep in the fridge for some time, so I don't think it's worth cooking a smaller piece.

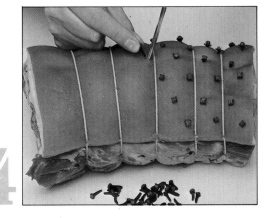

Stick cloves through the skin part of the joint. You may have to make holes with a skewer first to make it easier.

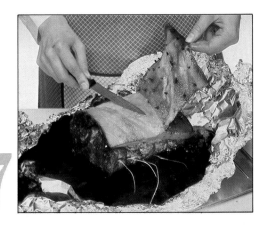

Take the joint out of the oven and unwrap it. Slide a small, sharp knife under the skin while it is still hot, and cut and pull it away from the fat.

2 Crush 1–2 tbsp juniper berries in a mortar. If you don't have one, place berries in a small polybag (to stop them rolling all over the place) and crush with a rolling pin.

3 Poke the crushed juniper berries well into the bacon with your fingers where you can, or make incisions if it is rolled so tightly that you can't get your fingers right in.

5 Crush 1–2 tbsp whole allspice berries in a mortar and press the meat on to them as firmly as possible to cover every part of the joint except for the skin.

6 Put the meat on a large rectangle of foil. Spoon the contents of a 1 lb (500 g) can of treacle all over the joint. Wrap completely in foil. Bake at Gas mark 1, 275°F, 140°C for 4 to 5 hours, according to size (about 1 hour per 1 lb/500 g).

8 Sprinkle the fatty surface with demerara sugar, and wrap the joint in foil again.

9 Put the joint on a plate with a board on top and weight it down with bags of flour, magazines or books. Leave overnight. Unwrap and sprinkle a little extra sugar on to the fat. Serve cut into very thin slices.

Elisabeth Luard's Cassoulet

'The French classic, cassoulet is quite simply the creature of its maker. Its creation is a balance of habit, necessity, availability and, as with all the best peasant cooking, the special genius of the cook!' enthuses Elisabeth Luard.

Cookery writer Elisabeth has lived abroad for many years and so gained an intimate knowledge of the cuisines of Europe – especially France, Spain and Italy. Elisabeth is also well known as a wildlife painter.

'I first learnt how to make cassoulet from my lovely French friend Madame Escrieu when I lived with a young family in Languedoc, southern France.

'Cassoulet is a wonderful recipe if you're planning to feed a crowd: this recipe will feed ten people with respectable appetites. Although the cooking time seems long, the recipe needs very little attention. Preparing the meats and layering them with the cooked beans takes about 40 minutes and, once in the oven, the cassoulet won't come to much harm if the meal is delayed. If you prefer to cook it the day before, cool and keep it in the fridge overnight. Bring to room temperature and reheat, uncovered, at Gas

'Reap the rewards of long, slow cooking with this wonderfully warming French bean casserole'

mark 4, 350°F, 180°C, for 1½ hours.

'Perhaps not surprisingly, cassoulet is one of those recipes that always provokes great controversy. There are as many recipes as there are cooks – but I put my money on this one! To obtain the best and tastiest cassoulet you need to choose plump white haricot beans and simmer them with belly pork, onions, cloves, garlic and herbs so they absorb the flavours during the first cooking. Sautéed duck or goose, lean pork and tasty sausage are layered in the beans and add their own distinctive end result. Traditionally, preserved goose or duck would be used, but the modern cook can use duck portions available from supermarkets. Enrich and spice the bean mixture with thickly sliced chorizo or pepperoni sausage. The fat within the sausage melts during the long, slow second cooking and is absorbed by the beans, adding the most wonderful flavour to every single one! Madame Escrieu would sometimes add fresh sausages to her cassoulet – coarse-textured, Toulouse pork sausage is regarded as the very best, but fresh, premium pork sausages will give a similar result. Like the French, vary the ingredients depending on availability.

'Cassoulet is traditionally made in a *toupin* – a large earthenware casserole with a curved base so the beans don't get caught in the corners. The pork rind is spread in the base, fat side uppermost, so the beans don't stick to the bottom. The beans and meat are layered alternately with the tomatoes and onions in the centre, so the beans can absorb the various flavours. Breadcrumbs on the top cook to a golden crust which is stirred into the beans.

'Now you'll reap the reward of your patience. To serve cassoulet, break through the crust and spoon down into the layers. (You find the duck is so tender, the meat just falls off the bone and the beans will be deliciously creamy.) You can give everyone a little duck, sausage and, of course, a good helping of beans. Serve with a fresh green salad and strong red wine.'

SERVES 10
INGREDIENTS:

FOR THE FIRST COOKING:
2 lb (1 kg) white haricot beans
1 lb (500 g) thick end belly pork
1 large onion spiked with 6 cloves
2 carrots, sliced
3 cloves garlic, peeled
small bunch fresh herbs (parsley, thyme, rosemary, bay leaf)
6 black peppercorns, crushed
FOR THE SECOND COOKING:
2 duck portions
1 lb (500 g) lean pork
3 cloves garlic, crushed
2 onions, chopped
1 lb (500 g) fresh premium pork sausages
2 large beefsteak tomatoes or 1 × 14 oz (397 g) can tomatoes
8 oz (250 g) chorizo or pepperoni sausage
1 oz (25 g) fresh breadcrumbs
salt and pepper

1 Prepare the 'first cooking' ingredients. Pick over 2 lb (1 kg) white haricot beans, soak in cold water for a few hours or overnight. Cut rind from 1 lb (500 g) thick end belly pork and reserve. Cut meat into cubes, discarding any bones.

4 Meanwhile, prepare the meats from the 'second cooking' ingredients. Fry 2 duck portions gently in a frying pan without any oil until the fat begins to run. Increase the heat and cook until browned all over. Lift out duck and reserve.

7 Drain beans, reserving cooking liquor. Discard the clove-spiked onion and bunch of herbs. Reserve the pork rind.

10 Spoon over another layer of beans. Cut each duck portion in two and place on top. Thickly slice 8 oz (250 g) chorizo or pepperoni sausage and arrange over duck. Spoon over remaining beans. Add a ladleful of cooking liquid.

2 Drain beans, put in a large pan, cover with cold water. Add diced pork and rind, 1 large onion spiked with 6 cloves, 2 sliced carrots, 3 cloves garlic, small bunch fresh herbs and 6 black peppercorns, crushed. Bring to the boil.

3 Skim off the grey foam that rises. Boil for 10 min then reduce heat and simmer for 1 hour until beans are soft but still whole. Top up as necessary with boiling water.

5 Cut 1 lb (500 g) lean pork into large pieces, fry with 3 crushed cloves garlic in the duck fat. Lift out the pork and reserve.

6 Pour off and reserve all but 1 tbsp of the duck fat. Fry 2 chopped onions in the fat until softened, but not browned.

8 Start layering the cassoulet. Place the pork rind in the base of a deep, 8 pt (4 litre) casserole, fat side uppermost. Spoon one third of the bean mixture into the casserole.

9 Put all the lean pork on top, cover with another layer of beans, then 1 lb (500 g) whole, premium pork sausages. Spoon over 2 peeled and chopped beefsteak tomatoes, or 14 oz (397 g) canned tomatoes, and the fried onions.

11 Cover and cook at Gas mark 1, 275°F, 140°C for 2 hours. Uncover and add a little boiling water if the beans look dry. Cook for a further 1 hour.

12 Sprinkle on top 1 oz (25 g) breadcrumbs. Trickle 1 tbsp reserved, melted duck fat over the crumbs. Increase oven temperature to Gas mark 3, 325°F, 160°C. Cook for 30 min. Stir crust into beans, with seasoning. Cook for 30 min.

Peter Boizot's Four Seasons Pizza

'The first time I ate pizza it made an immediate impact. It was colourful to look at, fragrant to smell, succulent to taste. The pizza became, from that moment, a food which nurtured my body and my pocket for many years.'

Peter Boizot opened the first branch of PizzaExpress in 1965. Until then he had found that in London it was very difficult to find a pizza worth the name.

'People would tell me that you could find a good pizza here or there, so I made special pilgrimages to this or that restaurant but seldom with any satisfaction. Each time the pizza failed to appear on the menu, or to come up to my expectations, I would stalk out muttering that the only thing to do was to set up my own pizzeria.

'One evening, after we'd been offered three inches of dreary dough, a scraping of tacky cheese and a few sad olives, I had my usual grouse. A friend who was with me (and probably weary of these performances) seized her chance. "You're always talking about it," she said, "go and do it!" So I did. Immediately I set about finding premises, a pizza oven, a pizzaiolo – the pizza chef – to

'Creative cooking with basic ingredients – colourful to look at, fragrant to smell, succulent to taste'

work it, a staff of genuine Neapolitans, and securing a supply of mozzarella – the essential cheese for pizza.

'Making a pizza from basic ingredients is very satisfying. Ordinary plain flour is best – the authentic flavour and feel comes from the combination of plain flour and yeast, but wholemeal flour can be used for a "brown" pizza. Make sure the flour is reasonably warm. If your flour barrel sits in a cool larder, bring out what you need in plenty of time.

'Always sift the flour – this distributes the air and you are already on your way to producing a light dough. It is so easy to forget the salt – I suggest you put the amount you need into the flour as you measure it on the scales – then sift them together. Fresh yeast and dried yeast are equally suitable but because it is a living substance, the fresh kind seems to have much more character.

'It is a case of "clear the decks" when you are going to make pizza – and the more uncluttered space you can give yourself to work in, the better. Make one very large pizza, or halve the doughball for two 9in (23cm) ones.

'Inventiveness can reach its peak when cooking pizza. Simplicity and balance are the keynotes; restrict the amount of ingredients used on each, and make sure they blend or contrast. Also, when it goes into the oven, the pizza should look underfilled rather than overfilled. I have sometimes been carried away – another olive, a little more cheese, and so on . . . until the dough begins to expand and cook, cheese melts and bubbles, and before you know where you are, the pizza has overflowed in the oven.

'Orvieto Secco (a dry white wine) is well matched to the Four Seasons Pizza though any *vino da tavola* (Italian table wine) is good and it does no harm to cool it slightly.

'Let your own fancy have full rein when you are your own pizzaiolo – making the simplest, most classic or most unusual pizza – just keep experimenting!'

SERVES 2
INGREDIENTS:

FOR THE DOUGH:
½ oz (15g) fresh yeast or 2 teaspoons dried yeast
1 level teaspoon sugar
8 oz (250g) plain flour, sifted
1½ level teaspoons salt
FOR THE SAUCE:
1 small onion
1 clove garlic
olive oil
8 oz (226g) can Italian plum tomatoes
1 tablespoon tomato purée
salt and black pepper
1 bay leaf, crushed
oregano
FOR THE TOPPING:
3 oz (75g) mozzarella cheese
2 oz (50g) mushrooms
2 oz (50g) pepperoni sausage
4 anchovies
6 black olives
20 capers

With your fingers squeeze ½oz (15g) fresh yeast into ¼pt (150ml) tepid water, with 1 level tsp sugar, and swirl until dissolved. If using dried yeast, sprinkle onto liquid, whisk in with a fork, then stand until a froth develops. Meanwhile sift 8oz (250g) plain flour into a mixing bowl with 1½ level tsp of salt.

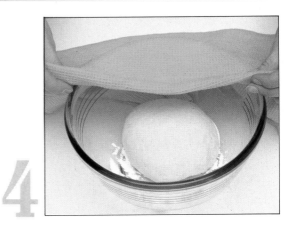

When the dough is soft and supple, rinse the mixing bowl with cold water, dry it, sprinkle in a touch of flour and place the doughball in it. Cover with a damp cloth and allow to stand somewhere warm for approximately one hour. Place clear of draughts but not in direct heat.

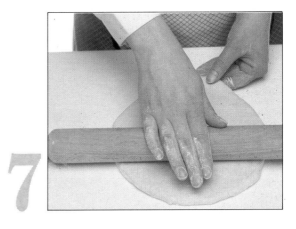

By now the dough should be roughly twice its original size, so gently lift it up and punch it down again. Leave under an upturned bowl for 10 to 20min. Preheat the oven to Gas mark 8, 450°F, 230°C. Use one hand only to roll out the dough to a large circle, exerting a light pressure on the rolling pin.

Pour the yeast mixture into the sifted flour and salt. Work the flour and liquid together until they bind as a dough. Sprinkle the work surface generously with flour. Tip the dough on to the work surface and scrape off any which is sticking to the bowl.

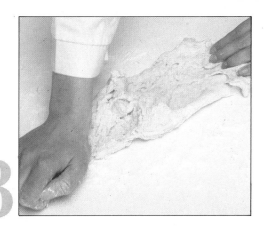

Begin kneading. You may already have an established method of kneading dough, but if you have never done this before I suggest you pull the far edge of the dough towards the centre with one hand and push it down and away from you with the heel of the other hand. Continue kneading for about 5 min.

For the tomato sauce, finely chop 1 small onion and crush a clove of garlic. Soften for about 10 min in 1 tbsp olive oil, do not brown. Add the can of Italian plum tomatoes, 1 tbsp tomato purée, salt, black pepper, a crushed bay leaf and a sprinkling of oregano. Simmer until you have a thickish sauce.

The Four Seasons Pizza requires 3 oz (75 g) sliced mozzarella cheese, 2 oz (50 g) sliced mushrooms, 2 oz (50 g) sliced pepperoni sausage and 4 anchovies. If you find anchovies too salty soak them in a little milk first. Mozzarella cooks well, becoming soft and stringy. Pepperoni sausage is oily so slice thinly.

When you have rolled out the dough, put the circle on to a greased baking tray and pat it gently into shape. Pinch a rim around the edge. The dough will expand again during cooking — not much, but enough to produce a hefty crust if the uncooked dough is not flattened thinly and evenly.

Spread the tomato sauce over. Arrange the mozzarella, mushrooms, pepperoni and anchovies on separate quarters. Dot with 6 black olives and about 20 capers. Add salt, pepper and a little oil (not too much oil on the pepperoni, or too much salt on the anchovies). Cook for 15 min, until well risen and golden.

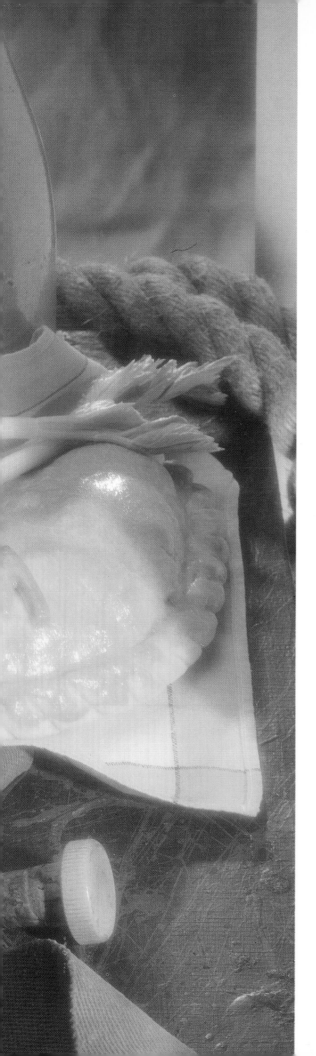

Theodora Fitzgibbon's Cornish Pasties

There's so much controversy surrounding the traditional Cornish pasty that the best person to turn to for an authentic recipe is the best known, and probably the most prolific of all the 'British Cookery' specialists, cookery writer Theodora Fitzgibbon. She says, 'It's really quite odd that something as simple as a Cornish pasty should create such argument. Some people feel that the only way to make them is to fold the pastry around the filling, then seal and crimp the edges across the top – I think this is a more modern version. Others will argue that a true pasty has the join underneath, but I prefer the version with the pastry folded flat over the filling and the edges sealed with a fork or twisted into a rope. Whichever way you choose, the important thing is to seal the edges together really well, so none of the lovely savoury juices run out.

'Pasties have been the staple food in Cornwall for centuries and were traditionally served as a packed lunch for the local tin miners, fishermen and school-children. The pastry obviously had to be firm enough to withstand travelling, just wrapped in a cloth, but not so hard that the pasty could be dropped down a mine shaft without breaking – an old Cornish joke! The very old recipes were those with the side join; the resulting thick edge or crust

'The most convenient fare, a marvellous meal in one'

131

was used as a 'handle' which helped keep the pasty free from the dust and dirt of the mine. Cooks always added an initial in the corner (diners would begin eating from the other end), so that if lunch or 'crib' (food time) was interrupted, the owner knew which pasty was his! It also meant that if anyone had a different filling there would be no confusion.

'Almost anything can go into a pasty as long as it's moist, and cut small enough to allow the pasty to be eaten without a knife and fork. Also, all the ingredients should be added raw – and filling that is cut small will finish cooking at the same time as the pastry. The old recipes always contained thinly sliced turnips, but original Cornish pasty recipes really were flexible, and you'd add whatever you had to hand – lean beef or lamb, chopped onion and potato, and a sprinkling of chopped herbs. When times were especially hard the cook would cut down on the meat or leave it out altogether.'

When searching out information, Theodora and her husband, George Morrison, an archivist, set off to Cornwall and stayed with friends. 'You learn so much more chatting to the locals over a pint of beer. People often tease me and say that my middle name should be "research" – I love to find out about all sorts of recipes and styles of cooking. My Cornish grandmother's handwritten recipe book has been a great help, too.

'I think out of all my books, I most enjoyed working in the West Country. The people were so friendly and the background information so interesting. Being an archivist, my husband knows so many people who can put me in touch with others who are always ready to lend a hand.'

Theodora has written more than 30 books, plus two autobiographies and two novels. She was former Cookery Editor on *Homes and Gardens*, *Harpers Bazaar* and *Vogue*.

SERVES 4
INGREDIENTS:

FOR THE PASTRY:
8 oz (250 g) butter or block margarine
1 lb (500 g) plain flour
a generous pinch of salt
FOR THE FILLING:
2 medium-sized potatoes
1 medium-sized onion
1 medium-sized turnip
a few sprigs of fresh herbs – thyme, parsley or rosemary
salt and pepper
1 lb (500 g) lean stewing beef or lamb
beaten egg to glaze

Rub 8 oz (250 g) butter or block margarine into 1 lb (500 g) plain flour mixed with a generous pinch of salt. Using a palette knife, stir in 8 tbsp cold water – add a very little more water if necessary to bring the dough together. Knead lightly to a smooth dough. Leave to one side in a cool place.

Place spoonfuls of the vegetable mixture on each pastry circle so that the mixture is on only one half of the pastry. Top with the thinly sliced turnip then the diced meat and level the mixture so that it evenly fills half the pastry circle, but leaving a ¾ in (2 cm) border.

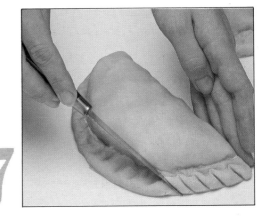

Crimp the edge by pinching with fingertips all round the pastry edge. Draw the back of a small knife across the edge at a 45° angle at ½ in (1 cm) intervals to give a rope effect.

Peel the potatoes and cut into ½in (1 cm) dice. Peel and chop the onion. Peel and thinly slice the turnip. Chop or snip the fresh parsley, thyme or rosemary. Place the vegetables and herbs in a bowl. Season. Trim away the fat from the meat and cut into ½in (1 cm) dice, place on a plate. Season.

Knead the pastry lightly and roll out on a surface dusted with flour. Roll the pastry out thinly until about 19 in (48 cm) square. Cut out four large circles using a 9 in (23 cm) plate as a guide. Reserve trimmings.

Brush the edges of the pastry with water and carefully fold the pastry over the filling until the edges meet. Press the edges together well with your fingertips to seal tightly.

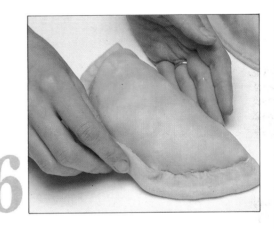

Brush the top of the pastry edge with water and fold it back on itself towards the filling. Press the folded edges together to seal tightly.

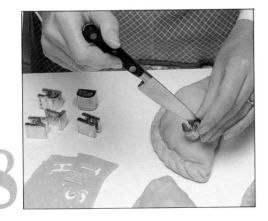

Re-roll the pastry trimmings and cut out initials, if liked, with small cutters or freehand with a small knife. Brush one end of each pasty with water and press an initial on the corner. Make a small cut in the top of each pastry for the steam to escape. Place on a greased baking sheet.

Bake the pasties in a moderately hot oven, Gas mark 6, 400°F, 200°C, for 20 min until the pastry is pale golden. Reduce the oven temperature to Gas mark 4, 350°F, 180°C; brush the pasties with beaten egg to glaze and cook for a further 20 min, until crisp and golden.

DESSERTS

Anne Willan's Chocolate Profiteroles

An economics graduate brought up in Yorkshire seems an unlikely person to set up a cookery school in Paris. However, Anne Willan did just that in 1975, when she opened the Ecole de Cuisine La Varenne. After reading economics at Cambridge, Anne switched her attention to food – 'because I like practical subjects and I like to eat!' – and went on to study, and later teach, at the Cordon Bleu school in London. A spell at the Ecole du Cordon Bleu in Paris led to her winning the school's highest award, the Grande Diplôme.

It was Anne's enthusiasm for French cooking and her realization that in France, cookery is learnt either at home from *maman* or in very formal trade schools or apprentice-ships (where students are not encouraged to ask questions) that made her feel she had a contribution to make. She felt there was a need for a cookery school with a more sympathetic attitude, where emphasis was given to a feeling and flair for food as well as to recipes.

Consequently, at La Varenne, classes are small (about ten in each of the two kitchens) and students gather around

'I can't get over my mistrust of the power of plain eggs to transform gluey butter, flour and water paste into crisp balloons of pastry with hollow centres, so neatly designed to hold rich fillings'

the chef, working and watching carefully, but able to ask questions and make contributions. Students cook a full menu, which they eat with their tutors at lunch and dinner so they have the opportunity to criticize and become used to discussing food seriously and at length. Lessons are grouped by subject, so students learn basic techniques, which they combine later in the course in more complicated dishes.

There is a maximum of 40 students and most of them come from other countries – the United States, Britain, South Africa. The whole philosophy behind La Varenne is to make French cookery more accessible to people from 'abroad', so classes are held in English and the staff are open-minded, friendly and helpful, finding places for students to live and, encouraging them in their work, especially if they are studying full time as well as at the cookery school.

As Anne says, 'Our aim at La Varenne is to build confidence. We want students to understand methods and techniques and why they work. They learn to improvise, where corners can be cut . . . and where they can't! Time and labour are cut, but never standards. Most importantly, we want our cooks to regard recipes not just as blueprints to be strictly adhered to, but as free-form sketches from which to create their personal style.

'Choux pastry is just one of the lessons that make up the course. Once you've mastered the basic skills, you can use choux to make gâteaux, savoury dishes and the ever-popular *profiteroles au chocolat*. These are my father's favourite, and I serve them on special occasions because everyone loves them, especially children. Sometimes I serve a fresh raspberry sauce instead of the chocolate. Frankly, such fresh, crisp choux pastry with a rich, melting filling is rare outside the home kitchen.'

INGREDIENTS:

FOR THE CHOUX PASTRY:
3½ oz (110 g) plain flour
½ teaspoon salt
3 oz (75 g) butter
3 eggs, size 2 or 3
1 egg beaten with ½ teaspoon salt, to glaze
FOR THE FILLING:
6 egg yolks
4 oz (125 g) caster sugar
2½ oz (60 g) plain flour
¾ pt (450 ml) milk
1 vanilla pod
¼ pt (150 ml) double cream
2 tablespoons icing sugar
FOR THE CHOCOLATE SAUCE:
3½ oz (110 g) plain dessert chocolate
1 oz (25 g) butter
1 tablespoon rum, brandy or Grand Marnier

Sift 3½ oz (110 g) plain flour on to a piece of greaseproof paper. Put a scant ⅓ pt (185 ml) water, ½ tsp salt and 3 oz (75 g) butter in a large, heavy-based saucepan. Heat until the butter is melted, then bring to the boil.

With a wooden spatula, beat 2 eggs into the dough, one at a time, beating thoroughly after each addition. The dough should be warm enough to cook the eggs slightly. At first, the dough thickens, then it starts to thin down and look glossy.

Mark the dough with the prongs of a fork, so it will rise evenly – choux cracks as it puffs and will rise best if the cracks are in regular patterns. The choux will double in size as it is baked.

When the puffs are cooked, transfer them to a cooling tray immediately. While they are still warm, split them to release the steam, or poke them with a knife.

Take from the heat immediately, so the dough proportions are not altered by water evaporation. Immediately, tip in all the flour at once, so the flour cooks to a solid dough. If the flour is added little by little, it cooks into lumps.

Beat vigorously for a few seconds, using a wooden spatula, until the mixture is smooth and pulls away from the pan to form a ball. Beat again for ½ to 1 minute over a low heat to dry the mixture, but don't dry it for longer than this.

Lightly beat a third egg with a fork and add – little by little – until the dough is very shiny and falls easily from the spoon but keeps its shape. You may not need all of this reserved egg.

Put dough into a pastry bag fitted with a ⅜ in (1 cm) plain tube and pipe 1½ in (4 cm) mounds of dough well apart on a lightly buttered baking sheet. Don't overgrease the baking sheet or the choux will slide and become misshapen.

Use 1 egg beaten with ½ tsp salt to make the glaze. Brush each choux mound carefully with egg glaze, making sure it doesn't drip on to the baking tray. Bake in a moderately hot oven (Gas mark 6, 400°F, 200°C) for 20 to 25 minutes.

The puffs are cooked when they are firm and brown. Choux pastry invariably looks done before it is ready because it has browned; but it also has to dry, and must continue to dry in the oven for 5 to 10 minutes after it has browned.

For the filling, beat egg yolks with caster sugar and plain flour. Heat the milk with a vanilla pod until boiling. Pour on to egg mixture, whisking constantly. Bring to boil. Cook, whisking for 2 min. Cool. Whip cream with icing sugar and fold in.

For the chocolate sauce, melt the chocolate and 1 oz (25 g) butter in 5 tbsp water over a low heat, stirring occasionally. Do not boil. Stir in rum, brandy or Grand Marnier. Coat the profiteroles with chocolate sauce and serve.

Katie Stewart's Meringues

Katie Stewart's personal approach to food has always been brilliantly straightforward. She has never been one for fiddly or complicated recipes, and writes practically and with a very real understanding of her favourite subject.

'Cooking can be exasperating, but the *un*boring thing about it is that however much you cook, there's always something new to learn. And I'll "talk shop" with anyone,' she enthused. 'I love discussions about recipes, about techniques which explain why ingredients react in different ways – and I'm all for banishing as much culinary mystery as possible. It's this exchange of ideas that makes cooking enjoyable – and easier – and looking back, it's the reason why I always wanted to write for other cooks, to pass on the hints and tips I've discovered.'

Born in Scotland, Katie trained at Aberdeen's School of Domestic Science, as her mother and grandmother had done, then enrolled at Westminster College, London, where she took a catering course, and graduated with a Diploma. A year in France at the famous Cordon Bleu school preceded an exciting move to New York, as home

'Like every Scottish cook I know, I bake meringues in a falling oven heat – as a baker once taught me'

economist for Nestlé. After working, travelling and recipe-swapping in the States, she began her journalistic career in Britain, becoming particularly popular for her knack of incorporating 'useful hints' into her writing.

Imparting her meringue know-how, she commented: 'Perhaps it's because meringues, with their faint caramel colour and delicate flavour, seem such clever creations that many cooks dread preparing them! If you're careful at every stage, there's no problem. I admit I've a sweet tooth so I don't allow myself meringues as often as I'd like, but whenever there's a special occasion, they're definitely on the menu.

'The most manageable method, even if you're aiming for meringues by the dozen, is to work with only two eggs at a time. I do, and I use size 2 eggs. It's vital to keep yellow yolk traces out of the whites, to achieve the snowy, stiff peaks you're after. I always separate whites the day before so some of the moisture evaporates, giving a more concentrated solution of albumen, which, by my reckoning, equals better volume. Remember, older eggs are more acid and whisk up better than new-laid, which are alkaline.

'Successful-every-time meringues begin with a spotlessly clean bowl and whisk, so scald both with boiling water and then dry them thoroughly.

'A Stewart secret you're compelled to share is that damp sugar is fatal to the meringue exercise. For crisp meringue, the proportion of sugar is 2oz (50g) to each egg white. Where meringue is used to decorate a pie or pudding, the quantity of sugar is reduced to 1½oz (40g) per egg white to get a lighter mixture. For Pavlova, or if you like a soft, spongy centre, add 1tsp vinegar or lemon juice when folding in the sugar. For meringue shells, the easiest way to make them is by spooning them on to baking sheets, though you can pipe them into swirls or nest shapes. I often add finely ground almonds, roasted hazelnuts or walnuts. Use about 1oz (25g) ground nuts per egg white and fold into the whites when adding the second lot of sugar. Once made, meringue must be placed in the oven and baked at once or it will weep. I was taught by a baker that the best way to bake meringues was in a falling oven heat. In this way, the outside sets and the dropping temperature allows the meringues to dry out. Cooking meringues on a constant low temperature will cause the sugar to weep out and bubble on the baking sheet. I like to serve individual meringues with fruit salad, or sandwich two together with whipped cream – the perfect accompaniment.'

INGREDIENTS:

2 eggs
½ lemon
pinch of salt
pinch of cream of tartar (optional)
4oz (100g) caster sugar
½pt (300ml) double cream

Separate 2 eggs (preferably the day before cooking) and put whites into a whisking bowl – if you wipe it first with half a cut lemon, the acid will help give better volume and stabilize the foam. Some moisture will evaporate overnight, resulting in a stronger concentration of albumen, which will also help with the volume.

Weigh out 4oz (100g) caster sugar. I usually dry it on a baking sheet for 5 to 10min in the oven as it heats up, before whisking the egg whites. Crush any lumps and press through a sieve. Gradually add half the sugar, about 1tbsp at a time, and whisk whites back to their original stiffness after each addition.

Sprinkle with a little extra caster sugar. Place the sheets just above and just below the centre of the oven. Close the door and lower the temperature to Gas mark ¼, 200°F, 110°C. Wedge the door slightly ajar with the handle of a wooden spoon. Leave to dry for 2 hours, rotating the sheets occasionally.

2 The next day, when you are ready to make your meringues, firstly preheat the oven to cool (Gas mark 2, 300°F, 150°C), then grease two baking sheets with white cooking fat. Dust well with flour and tap sharply to remove any excess. If you prefer, line the sheets with nonstick baking parchment.

3 Add a pinch of salt to the egg whites (and a pinch of cream of tartar if you did not wipe the bowl with lemon), whisk lightly until frothy, then whisk faster until they form stiff, shiny peaks. Working by hand, you can feel when the whites are at the correct stage. Do not overwhisk, or they will become cotton-woolly.

5 Sprinkle on the remaining sugar and carefully fold into the egg whites, using a large metal spoon. Use a lifting and cutting movement, taking great care not to overmix or knock out the air at this stage, or the meringue will just collapse. The sugar should be well distributed throughout the foam.

6 The simplest method of shaping meringues is to use two metal tablespoons. Take a rounded spoonful of the mixture, scoop it out with the second spoon to form a neat oval shape, and let it fall on to the prepared baking sheets. Arrange 6 ovals neatly on each baking sheet.

8 Slip a palette knife under each meringue – if they are sufficiently baked, they should lift off the baking sheet easily. Turn the shells over on to their sides, turn off the oven heat and leave the meringues in the oven to dry for a further hour. When quite crisp and dry, the meringues will keep perfectly in an airtight tin.

9 Whisk ½pt (300ml) double cream until it holds its shape. Spread a little cream between each pair of meringues, then place them in paper cake cases. Place remaining cream in a large nylon piping bag fitted with a large star tube and pipe a continuous swirl of cream between each pair. Leave about 2 hours before serving.

Anne Willan's
Crème Caramel

Anne Willan, founder of the famous La Varenne cookery school in Paris, is also a busy mum! With her husband, a world banker, and two children to care for, she's as used to family catering as she is to the more exotic sort.

'My children have enjoyed Crème Caramel since infancy, so I often make one for family dinners in a 2 pt (1 litre) dish. For special dinners I make individual ones. Turned out on to small plates and decorated with strawberries and mint leaves, they look absolutely stunning! Yet Crème Caramel is so simple to make – it needs only four main ingredients, is easy, fast and can be made in advance.' And that's important because Anne is tremendously busy. La Varenne still occupies most of her time, but she is also often invited to teach at other people's cookery schools and is involved with the International Association of Cooking Schools. She also contributes a regular column to the *Washington Post* – a weekly menu complete with recipes and that all-important, confidence-building time plan. Consequently she spends a lot of time dashing between the USA and Paris.

'I can't imagine any flavour more popular than caramel combined with a satin-smooth vanilla custard'

CRÈME CARAMEL

At La Varenne, Anne is emphatic about teaching the principles that lie behind every recipe, because she's convinced that if you know *why* you are carrying out a certain process you can be confident of success. 'Properly made, Crème Caramel is a classic, smooth-textured combination of eggs and milk covered with a thin coating of liquid caramel. It is simple to make once you know why the various procedures are so important. A carefully balanced mixture of eggs and milk will set to the desired jelly-like consistency when heated to a known temperature. This must be below the boiling point of water, but hot enough to cook the egg.

'I teach my students to stand the custard in a water bath or *bain-marie* to help regulate the cooking temperature. Otherwise, if the custard is heated above the egg setting point, many small holes will appear and the mixture becomes tough. This happens because the egg toughens and shrinks slightly, squeezing out the watery part of the milk and holding only the milk solids – giving a "curdled" custard.

'To avoid this disappointing result the water in the *bain-marie* should be scarcely bubbling. The correct cooking time is estimated from the moment the water starts to simmer, so the water in the *bain-marie*, with the dish in it, should be brought to the boil before putting it in the oven to cook. Then it is simply a matter of making sure the water continues to simmer and keeping it topped up with hot water.

'If you follow these basic guidelines you'll find the caramel easy to make with perfect results every time. And you don't need to leave it to the day of the party. It can be made up to 48 hours in advance, covered with cling film and kept in the fridge – it doesn't freeze. Don't unmould it until just before serving, though, or all the delicious caramel runs off the top!'

SERVES 4
INGREDIENTS:
FOR THE CARAMEL:
2 fl oz (50 ml) water

3½ oz (100 g) sugar
FOR THE CRÈME:
1 pt (600 ml) milk

1 vanilla pod

2½ oz (75 g) sugar

2 eggs

2 egg yolks

Set oven to moderate, Gas mark 4, 350°F, 180°C. Heat 2 fl oz (50 ml) water and 3½ oz (100 g) sugar until dissolved. Use a heavy-based pan, and heat gently over a fairly low heat. Stir until all the sugar has dissolved in the water. Warm a 2 pt (1 litre) soufflé dish or a heatproof mould in oven for a few min.

Remove the dish or mould from the oven. When the bubbles in the caramel have subsided, pour it into the mould and immediately turn the mould round to coat the base and sides evenly. The caramel will still be very hot, so hold the dish carefully with oven gloves. Leave to cool and set.

Strain the custard into the prepared mould. If the milk is too hot it will dissolve too much of the caramel, leaving only a thin layer instead of a thick one. Straining the milk holds back any bits of unmixed egg, bits of milk skin and vanilla pod. Lift out the vanilla pod, rinse, dry, then store ready to use again.

2

When the syrup is completely clear, bring to the boil. Do not stir while boiling or the sugar may crystallize. There's no need to 'wash down' the stray sugar crystals – they usually burn or darken and if they fall into the caramel, won't crystallize it.

3

Boil steadily to a golden brown caramel. Some people like it pale, sugary and tasteless, but I like it dark, when it just begins to smoke. Don't cook any longer or it will taste bitter. It's best to remove the pan from the heat when the mixture is just lighter than the colour you require. Now work quickly.

5

Scald 1 pt (600 ml) milk: put it into a medium-sized saucepan with a vanilla pod. Bring to the boil, stirring with a wooden spoon. Remove from the heat, cover and leave to infuse for 10 to 15 min. Add 2½ oz (75 g) sugar and stir until completely dissolved.

6

Beat 2 eggs and 2 egg yolks until mixed. Stir in the hot milk mixture. The whole eggs in Crème Caramel bind the mixture so that it sets to a delicate yet firm custard which will turn out neatly. Allow mixture to cool slightly, for about 5 min.

8

Put the mould in a water bath and bring water to the boil on top of the stove. Almost any pan will do for a water bath, provided it is wide enough to hold the dish and deep enough for a minimum 2 in (5 cm) of water. When boiling, transfer water bath and dish to the oven and cook for 40 to 50 min. Remove from oven.

9

When a knife inserted near the centre of the custard comes out cleanly, it needs to be taken from the water bath. Leave to cool. Not more than an hour before serving, run a knife around the crème and turn it out on to a serving dish. It can be made up to 48 hours ahead and kept covered in the refrigerator.

Bernice Hurst's Perfect Cheesecake

Bernice Hurst became an author 'by accident', and it all started with cheesecakes . . . She was born and brought up in New York, where cheesecakes were a regular meal-time feature. So it wasn't until Bernice came over to Britain and settled in a small village that she realized their novelty value: 'The cheesecakes I made were quite unlike any of the desserts people were used to. I was asked for recipes and was given other recipes to try by family and friends. I played around with them, making new and interesting variations. And then it dawned on me that people were very keen on cheesecakes, but they just didn't know how to make them, so a book on the subject suddenly seemed to be a really good idea.

'I did a synopsis, took it round to various publishers, but got lots of rejections. My husband Ray is a journalist and it was his idea to go ahead and publish the book ourselves. We couldn't afford to do a hardback version, so we decided on a small-format paperback with a careful selection of well tested and presented recipes. A local printer agreed to print the book for us, my father-in-law

'Contrasts in texture – a crusty base, smooth filling and silky topping – are the hallmarks of the perfect cheesecake'

did the illustrations, and a neighbour designed the cover (in return for a bottle of whisky). We started off selling to local shops, but then things really took off!'

Bernice chose this recipe from that first little book, *The Perfect Cheesecake*: 'To me this is the perfect cheesecake because it has great texture. I love the contrast between the crusty base, smooth filling and silky topping. I find baked cheesecake less cloying than crumb-based, uncooked ones.'

But Bernice believes in flexibility. 'If it's what you like, it's right. If you'd prefer this with a crumb base, just make sure they're only lightly coated with butter so the base stays crisp, neither soft nor solid. Most cheesecake recipes are interchangeable. If you like fruit with your cheesecake, bake the case blind and add a layer of fruit before the cheese mixture. You won't see it until it's sliced so it'll come as a lovely surprise!

'This particular cheesecake is typically American because of the soured cream.

'I prefer to make cheesecakes at least a day in advance because I think they need time to firm up. Personally, I like it best chilled, but if you can't bear it "straight from the fridge" serve it at room temperature – that's lovely, too.'

So why is Bernice so sure she has the recipe for perfection? 'All my recipes have been thoroughly kitchen-tested,' she says, 'and then subjected to stringent "taste tests" by family and friends.' Members of the enthusiastic taste panel are Bernice's husband and three children, Sara, Joel and Sam. 'To be honest, though, my family has been a bit over-exposed to cheesecakes in the past, so now I save it to serve as a rare treat!'

SERVES 10–12
INGREDIENTS:

FOR THE BASE:
2½ oz (65 g) butter
2½ oz (65 g) caster sugar
1 egg
8 oz (250 g) plain flour
FOR THE FILLING:
1½ lb (750 g) cream cheese
8 oz (250 g) caster sugar
1 teaspoon grated lemon rind
1 tablespoon lemon juice
3 eggs
FOR THE TOPPING:
8 fl oz (250 ml) soured cream
1 teaspoon vanilla essence

Cheesecake bases are often made with crumbs moistened with melted butter. For this baked cheesecake, egg-enriched pastry is best. Place 2½ oz (65 g) softened butter and 2½ oz (65 g) caster sugar in a large bowl; beat with a wooden spoon until the mixture is light in colour and fluffy in texture.

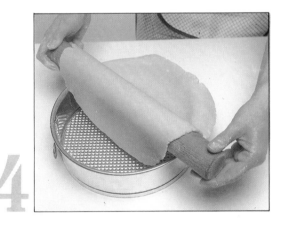

Handle pastry as little as possible. Roll out on a lightly floured surface to a circle large enough to line the base and sides of a loose-bottomed 9 in (23 cm) springform cake tin. Wrap pastry over rolling pin and lift into cake tin. Press pastry into base of tin and up against edges of tin with your fingers.

Beat the cheese mixture with a wooden spoon until really smooth. In a basin, lightly whisk together 3 eggs. Then add the eggs gradually to the cheese mixture, beating continuously between each addition until evenly blended.

Lightly beat one egg. Gradually add it to the creamed butter and sugar, in the bowl, beating continuously so that the egg is incorporated and the mixture remains light and fluffy. Preheat oven to Gas mark 8, 450°F, 230°C.

Sift 8oz (250g) plain flour into the mixture and beat in with a wooden spoon. It will form a stiff dough which leaves the sides of the bowl clean. Turn out and shape into a round.

Using a sharp knife, trim the pastry so that it comes only three quarters of the way up the sides of the tin. Bake in the centre of the oven for 5min. The very hot temperature will 'set' the pastry and form the case. Remove from the oven.

To make filling, place 1½lb (750g) cream cheese in a large bowl. Full-fat soft cheese is best; medium-fat cheeses, such as ricotta, and other curd cheeses are also suitable. Weigh out 8oz (250g) caster sugar and add all but 2tbsp to the cheese. Add 1tsp grated lemon rind and 1tbsp lemon juice.

Pour the mixture into the pastry case. It should come to no more than ¼in (5mm) from the top of the pastry case. Bake it for 10min in the centre of the oven, then reduce the temperature to Gas mark 2, 300°F, 150°C and bake for 30min. The mixture should only just feel firm in the centre.

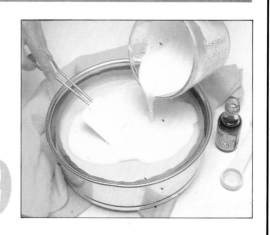

For the topping, beat 8floz (250ml) soured cream with 1tsp vanilla essence and the remaining 2tbsp sugar. Gently spread over the cheesecake and bake for a further 10min. Remove from the oven, allow to cool. Leave to mature overnight. You can serve this cheesecake at room temperature or chilled.

Raymond Blanc's Floating Islands

There are so many brilliant chefs now working in this country that it seems absurd that any of them should be titled 'Britain's superchef'. Perhaps this accolade has been given because Raymond Blanc, who is not yet 40, is quite a phenomenon. Not only is the food at his Oxfordshire restaurant creatively wonderful, praised by all who can afford to eat there (the restaurant is one of the most expensive in the country) but Raymond inspires everyone with his enthusiasm. And, amazingly, his talent is entirely his own. He has never had a cookery lesson, nor did he train under a great chef. He's the most professional amateur cook there is.

Is being called 'the best' an awful responsibility? 'Yes', says Raymond, 'I'm now there to be shot down. There's a danger in superlatives. People come to my restaurant expecting not food but a miracle! But no, it's lovely that Le Manoir aux Quat' Saisons was voted the best restaurant as soon as it opened.

'When I cook there is always an idea in my head which I follow until I get it right. If you are the same, if you are

'All you need in the fridge is milk and 10 eggs to make one of my favourite puddings.'

determined, say, that a mousse will be airy and light, you will cook better than some chefs who have been trained for five years but do not truly care.

'Good cooking is not elaborate. My style is really light not because of health (and no moral issue should be attached to eating) but because a meal is destroyed if it is too rich. I can't bear food that is like an overdressed person or an overdecorated room. Fundamental beauty is what I search for. "Buy good ingredients" is the golden rule – but it's up to you. You must not think of cooking as a cosmetic treatment for poor food.

'When I go out to dinner at a private house I really enjoy a simple joint, perfectly roasted. I believe that simple basics, like real vanilla custard, need to be rediscovered by home cooks. Once you have mastered custard you have an enormous repertory – it's the basis of the best ice creams, and puddings like bavarois.

'It's also the base of one of my favourite dishes, which we call Iles flottantes. I love it because it's part of my childhood and something French people enjoy all their lives; fifty million of us eat it every year! It's the most traditional French pudding there is, a delicious classic, simple dish found in homes, small brasseries and great restaurants alike.'

SERVES 4–6
INGREDIENTS:
FOR THE MERINGUE ISLANDS:
2 vanilla pods
1¾ pt (1 litre) milk
6 egg whites
12 oz (375 g) caster sugar
FOR THE CUSTARD:
10 egg yolks
3 oz (75 g) caster sugar
FOR THE DECORATION:
1 oz (25 g) flaked almonds
2 tablespoons icing sugar
FOR THE CARAMEL:
3½ oz (85 g) caster sugar

Split 2 vanilla pods lengthways to release the seeds. Put 1¾ pt/ 1 litre) milk in a large frying pan, add vanilla pods and bring to the boil. Reduce heat and simmer for 5 min. Remove pan from heat, and take out vanilla pods.

Hold the spoon just above the milk, reheat until it is 'shivering', and slide the meringue into it with the second spoon. Continue to shape meringues, cooking about 6 at a time. Cook for 2 min, turn over with back of spoon; cook for 2 min more.

Cook mixture over a medium heat until it has thickened. Do not boil or it will curdle. Stir constantly and watch for the moment when the custard coats the back of the spoon. The custard is ready when you run a finger through it and the line remains.

Not more than three hours before serving and preferably only one hour ahead, arrange drained, chilled meringues on custard. Lift each meringue with a palette knife and slide into place. Sprinkle caramelised almonds over meringues.

Whisk 6 egg whites until they form stiff, moist-looking peaks. Gradually add 12 oz (375 g) caster sugar, continuing to whisk until meringue has a shiny, firm texture. Stop whisking as soon as it reaches this stage or sugar will ooze out later.

Using two tablespoons dipped in hot water, take a spoonful of mixture and slide the bowl of the second spoon between the bowl of the first spoon and the meringue. Repeat so the meringue is on the first spoon again and now a smooth oval shape.

Remove cooked meringues with a slotted spoon and transfer to a small tray to drain. They will have minute specks of black on them because you have used real vanilla pods. Leave to drain (any milk on the meringues will spoil the custard). Chill.

Make the custard by whisking 10 egg yolks and 3 oz (75 g) caster sugar until pale yellow. Reheat the milk until almost boiling and gradually whisk in the egg mixture. When well mixed, pour into a saucepan.

Strain the custard into a serving bowl, or into individual bowls. Leave until cold and chill. Cover the surface with clingfilm to ensure a skin does not form. If you are in a hurry, you can use the custard warm.

Put 1 oz (25 g) flaked almonds on a baking sheet and sift 2 tbs icing sugar over. Grill under a moderate heat, turning once until the sugar has caramelised and the almonds are golden brown. Cool.

Use a pale-lined pan if possible, so you can judge colour of caramel. Pour in 2 fl oz (50 ml) water and add 3½ oz (85 g) to form a mound in the centre. Cook over medium heat, without stirring, until a dark rich caramel. Stand pan in cold water.

When caramel has stopped bubbling, quickly spoon over the meringues and almonds in zigzag lines. Do not spoon over the caramel too far in advance or it will not crackle – the caramel softens with standing.

155

Philippa Davenport's Lemon Meringue Pie

'A proper pudding like Lemon Meringue Pie shows how glorious puddings can be,' says cookery writer Philippa Davenport. 'They're meant to be rich in good things, but definitely not stodgy or heavy: that's what blemished their reputation. Although not the most sophisticated of fare, many puddings will grace a dining table, and are not too heavy to be eaten in the evening. To do full justice to a pudding, don't serve a first course, and serve only a light main course. If eaten in sensible quantities they'll fill you with a glow of contentment,' she adds, 'rather than leave you forced to take exercise or reduced to an after-dinner snooze!

'Light pies such as Lemon Meringue should be made with buttery pastry. Nowadays I make the pastry in a food processor and usually use a mixture of plain and whole-meal flours – I'm more health conscious than I used to be.

'When the pastry case is cooked my tip is to sprinkle on a tablespoon of toasted ground almonds, if I'm feeling rich; if I'm feeling poor it's a tablespoon of semolina! I may be hurried later on and have to add the filling while it's still

'A treat pudding – the contrast of crisp pastry, sharp lemon filling and sweet meringue topping is excellent'

hot – the almonds or semolina stop the moisture from the filling seeping through to the pastry, so there's less chance of the pie having a soggy bottom!

'I'm passionate about lemons, and this filling is genuinely lemony. It's wrong to think big lemons are better than small or medium ones – they often have a huge girth of pith whereas small ones have proportionately more juice. You can extract most juice by keeping lemons at room temperature, or slightly warm.

'If I just want to use the juice of a lemon, I always take off the zest first and freeze it away to use later for flavour or decoration. Citrus zesters (see step 3) are excellent – I much prefer to use one than grate my knuckles away on a grater. Use long strokes to pare away long, thin pieces, called julienne strips, for decoration. For this recipe, pare zest finely; it doesn't pick up any horrid pith, and the tiny pieces almost dissolve in cooking. By the way, a citrus zester makes a wonderful present.

'I like the meringue topping to be a soft honey colour. Whisk your egg whites with a rotary whisk – you just don't get the same volume from using an electric whisk. I try to remember I'm not a chef, I'm a human being, and although the arm exercise is good for me, I like to stop for a rest, so don't make it unnecessarily arm-aching. Whisking does become more difficult as the egg white gets stiffer, and you can tell when it's done entirely by "feel" – it becomes too difficult to whisk!

'To make the best puddings the cook's spirit must be generous. The freshest and best-quality ingredients – butter, eggs, sugar, cream, fresh fruits, dried fruits and nuts, high fruit-content jams – are essential. Use these ingredients lavishly, but be miserly with flour.

'Proper puddings are experiencing a return to popularity. They're no longer associated with the dull and heavy offerings served up by institutions. The true pudding tradition, for which the British are justly famous, is no longer in such serious danger of being lost. It's cheering for those who've always believed in simple excellence, and it reflects a growing awareness of the good sense of "getting back to basics" in all areas of home cooking.'

SERVES 6
INGREDIENTS:

FOR THE PASTRY:
2 oz (50 g) butter
2 oz (50 g) plain flour
2 oz (50 g) wholemeal flour
tiny pinch of salt
FOR THE FILLING:
3 lemons
4 oz (125 g) caster sugar
1½ oz (40 g) cornflour
1 oz (25 g) butter
2 egg yolks
FOR THE MERINGUE:
2 egg whites
4 oz (125 g) caster sugar

To make shortcrust pastry, rub 2 oz (50 g) butter, cut into small pieces, into 2 oz (50 g) plain flour and 2 oz (50 g) wholemeal flour with a tiny pinch of salt until the mixture resembles fine breadcrumbs. Add 3 tbsp water and mix, using a round-bladed knife, to form a soft dough. Chill for 10 min, in a polythene bag.

Whisk in the remaining water and cook over a medium heat until the mixture thickens and comes to the boil. Let it boil for 1 min, then remove it from the heat and beat in 1 oz (25 g) butter.

Whisk the 2 egg whites in a large, clean, grease-free bowl, until just past foamy – they don't have to be stiff before you add the sugar (see step 8). I prefer to use a rotary whisk to do this.

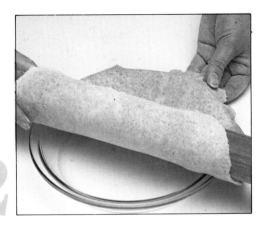

Roll out the pastry thinly; line a pie plate with sloping sides and a generous rim 6 in (15 cm) across the base and 8 in (20 cm) across the top, and trim. Cover with greaseproof paper. Weigh with baking beans and bake blind at Gas mark 6, 400°F, 200°C for 15 min. Remove paper and beans and bake for 10 min.

For the filling, pare away, or finely grate the zest of 3 lemons into a small saucepan. Add 4 oz (125 g) caster sugar, 1½ oz (40 g) cornflour, and a little water from ½ pt (300 ml) cold water. Mix together to make a smooth paste.

Squeeze the juice from 2 of the lemons, depending on juiciness. Measure 5 tbsp and beat into saucepan. Separate 2 eggs, add egg yolks one at a time to the lemon mixture, beat well. Set to one side to cool.

Spoon the cooled lemon filling into the pastry shell, adding more sugar if too tart. There is less chance of pastry becoming soggy if lemon filling is completely cold. Or you could sprinkle pastry with 1 tbsp toasted ground almonds or semolina. Preheat oven to Gas mark 2, 300°F, 150°C.

Gradually add 4 oz (125 g) caster sugar (about a third at a time) and continue whisking until the meringue mixture is stiff. It should be glossy and stand up in peaks.

Spread the meringue over the filling, taking it to the very edge of the pastry rim. Bake the pie in the centre of the oven for 50 to 60 min, until the top of the meringue has dried out to a crisp honey beige. Cool the pie for at least 20 min before serving.

Sarah Nops's Cold Lemon Soufflé

'People are always asking me how to get cold lemon soufflé to rise,' says Cordon Bleu Cookery School Principal, Sarah Nops. 'The truth is, you don't have to! As with all cold soufflés, the secret behind its light, fluffy risen look is to get as much air into the mixture as you can, then pour it into a dish with its sides extended by a greaseproof paper collar. Once the gelatine is set, the soufflé holds its shape, so you can peel away the paper collar.'

Cordon Bleu-trained, Sarah says her first cooking memories go back to making flour and water rolls in Ireland when she could barely reach the kitchen table! Much later, in 1974, having taught at Cordon Bleu, Sarah became Principal. 'People used to be terribly precise about minute decorating details, but really, life's too short to worry about the exact size of your cream rosettes. Yes, it's important to make the food look good, but with something like this lemon soufflé, it's much better to put all your efforts into perfecting your whisking technique to make a really full fluffy mixture ... and there are plenty of tricks to make it easy.

**'A Cordon Bleu classic –
sumptuously elegant and guaranteed for success'**

COLD LEMON SOUFFLÉ

'But first, a few minutes spent making a good paper collar will make all the difference to the end result. Make the collar by wrapping a large piece of folded greaseproof paper around the dish, following the instructions, so that it's at least 2 in (5 cm) above the rim. Tie it up tightly with string, or the soufflé mixture will trickle between the dish and the paper, then shape the collar into a good smooth round.'

Back to technique . . . 'Whisking the eggs over a bowl of hot water speeds up the process and creates maximum bulk – but be careful not to let the bottom of the whisking bowl touch the hot water otherwise the mixture will overheat and cook! If you don't have a hand whisk, but a fixed-head machine, then rinse the bowl in hot water before you begin. It's worth persevering with the whisking until the egg mixture is really thick and creamy, and resembles double cream. On the other hand, the cream to be folded in should be quite soft and fall back into the bowl in a thin ribbon, while piping cream needs to be whipped a little longer until it just holds its shape.

'Gelatine also seems to cause problems – people often shy away from recipes using it. All you need to remember is that unless it's properly dissolved, it won't set. Soak it in cold water until it resembles a sponge, then dissolve until it becomes a completely clear, straw-coloured liquid.

'At Cordon Bleu, we traditionally mask the top of the soufflé with a little whipped cream and pipe cream rosettes with a large star nozzle. We often suggest pressing chopped pistachios or ground ratafia biscuits around the edge of the soufflé, but I much prefer ground almonds.

'A delicious make-ahead dessert, the soufflé can be prepared early in the day, decorated 1 to 2 hours before serving and kept in the fridge until you're ready to serve. It really is the perfect end to a very special dinner – it's refreshingly tangy, very light, and very difficult to refuse!'

SERVES 6
INGREDIENTS:

½ oz (15 g) gelatine
2½ large lemons
3 eggs, size 1 or 2
6 oz (175 g) caster sugar
½ pt (300 ml) double or whipping cream
FOR FINISHING:
2 tablespoons ground almonds
¼ pt (150 ml) double or whipping cream
rind of 1 lemon
2 tablespoons caster sugar

1 Fold a piece of greaseproof paper, five times as deep as a 6 in (15 cm) No 2 soufflé dish, and long enough to go round with 4 in (10 cm) overlap, in half lengthways, then fold over deeply from folded edge. Tie round dish, with folded band at the bottom.

4 Continue whisking until the mixture is pale and creamy and very thick – it should resemble thick, unwhipped double cream – this may take 15 to 20 min. Remove the bowl from the saucepan and whisk until the exterior of the bowl is cold.

7 Turn into a metal bowl, or leave in glass bowl. Lower into a bowl of ice and water. Stir gently until it begins to thicken. Whisk egg whites separately until softly peaking. Remove bowl from ice, beat in 1 spoonful of egg white. Fold in remainder gently.

10 Lightly brown 2 tbsp ground almonds under the grill. Place the soufflé dish on a plate and press the ground almonds lightly around the side of the soufflé with a palette knife.

Place 2½ fl oz (70 ml) water in a small bowl, sprinkle ½ oz (15 g) gelatine over and stand for 5 min. Place the bowl in a small saucepan of hot water and heat gently, or microwave on medium setting (50%) for 1½ min, until dissolved and clear.

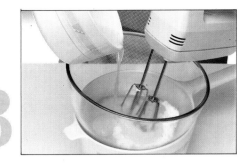

Grate rind and squeeze juice from 2½ large lemons. Warm the juice; reserve rind. Separate eggs, place yolks in a large bowl with 6 oz (175 g) caster sugar and reserve whites. Place bowl over (but not touching) hot water and whisk in warmed lemon juice.

Partially whip ½ pt (300 ml) double or whipping cream in a large bowl. The cream should fall back in a thin ribbon when the whisk is lifted out of the bowl.

Fold the whipped cream and grated lemon rind into the soufflé mixture using a flexible plastic spatula. Stir in the warm gelatine in a thin steady stream and mix well.

Pour the mixture into the prepared soufflé dish, smooth the top if necessary and place in the refrigerator to set.

Carefully remove the paper collar 1 to 2 hours before serving. Untie the string, press knife against the collar, then peel away the paper over the knife blade.

Lightly whip ¼ pt (150 ml) cream until just holding its shape. Spread a little over soufflé top and mark lightly with the back of a knife to create a lattice. Spoon remaining cream into a large piping bag with a star nozzle. Pipe rosettes around top edge.

Cut thin strips of peel from 1 lemon with a vegetable peeler and cut into thin needles. Boil in a little water for 2 min. Drain, add fresh water and 2 tbsp caster sugar, bring to boil, simmer gently until lightly candied. Drain, cool. Sprinkle over rosettes.

Martha Stewart's Pumpkin Pie

'As American as apple pie', runs the saying. But it's pumpkin pie which is the really individual American pie recipe. And it is one we gratefully borrow from the US at Hallowe'en, when hollowing out lanterns leaves masses of delicious chunks of pumpkin to cook.

Now Martha Stewart, bestselling American author, has come up with a beautiful new version of this old favourite. Pumpkin pie is the traditional dessert to complete American Thanksgiving dinners – the annual holiday to celebrate the Pilgrim Fathers' first harvest in the New World. Martha Stewart's pie has a festive, fun look with a pretty garland edging of pastry leaves. Extra leaves seem to float on top. 'Bake these separately and use to decorate the cooked pie, or they will disappear into the filling,' advises Martha.

Married with one daughter, Martha Stewart runs a catering business in Connecticut where she lives in an old farmhouse with acres of garden and orchards. So she's a very experienced cook and completely familiar with basic pie-making know-how. 'I've been making pastry crusts

'Pumpkin is the perfect autumn pie filling – mix with maple syrup and spices for America's favourite pie'

since I was a little girl and I think I've perfected the right proportion of butter, flour and water so the crust is light and tender, yet sturdy enough for pies. The pastry doesn't puff up, it makes a strong-sided pie and it browns nicely.'

Martha has a list of golden rules for pie making, first stressing that pastry should be made at speed. 'Ideally use a food processor – it should take 45 seconds maximum. Ingredients must be ice cold, pastry must be chilled thoroughly before rolling out quickly, evenly and with a minimum of flour.' She has tested pies and tarts in a range of different containers – tin, glass, crockery, aluminium. 'Best results were when we baked in the old-fashioned, lightweight tin pie-plates.'

Martha Stewart points out that pumpkin is a vegetable, and says its special quality is the way it lends itself to all sorts of flavours. She has several recipes, variously using honey, molasses, brown sugar (which gives a darker filling) and cinnamon, mace, nutmeg, ginger or allspice. Maple syrup, an American speciality, gives a really wonderful flavour. Real syrup is the product of boiling down sap from maples – don't use anything labelled 'maple-flavoured syrup'.

Martha has also tested canned and fresh pumpkin purée. She finds both excellent, the canned pulp giving a smoother finish, while the fresh purée has more texture. When dealing with large amounts of pumpkin from making lanterns, Martha makes a big batch of purée and freezes it in 12 oz (375 g) amounts 'ready for pie whenever I want it'. Another good get-ahead tip: 'Keep rounds of pastry rolled out and frozen between sheets of plastic wrap. The pastry needs only about 5 min to thaw enough to be pressed into a pie tin, filled and baked.' Yet another pretty idea for a party is to cook pumpkin pies in tartlet tins 'to make finger desserts'. So take advantage of this under-estimated vegetable and have fun making this delicious pie for Hallowe'en.

SERVES 6
INGREDIENTS:
FOR THE PASTRY:
10 oz (300 g) plain flour
¼ teaspoon salt
1 tablespoon caster sugar
6 oz (175 g) butter
FOR THE FILLING:
1½ lb (750 g) fresh pumpkin
½ pt (300 ml) milk
2 eggs
6 tablespoons maple syrup
3 tablespoons plain flour
1 teaspoon ground cinnamon
¼ teaspoon freshly grated nutmeg
¼ teaspoon ground ginger
pinch of salt
beaten egg to glaze
clotted cream to serve

Place 10 oz (300 g) plain flour, ¼ tsp salt and 1 tbsp caster sugar in the processor with 6 oz (175 g) butter, cut into pieces. Process for 10 seconds until the mixture resembles coarse crumbs. Or, place in a bowl and rub in the butter with the fingers.

Half-fill a large saucepan with water and bring to the boil. Place the pumpkin in a large colander or steamer, set over pan and check water is at least 1 in (2.5 cm) below the colander base. Cover and steam for 20 to 25 min or until soft. Cool.

Gently knead and roll out two thirds of the chilled pastry to an 11 in (28 cm) circle on a lightly floured surface. Lift pastry over a rolling pin and place in a deep 9 in (23 cm) pie plate.

Cut maple leaf shapes from remaining trimmings, mark veins, then place on a lightly greased baking sheet. Brush with beaten egg and cook separately at Gas mark 6, 400°F, 200°C for 5 min or until they have turned a pale golden brown.

Add 2 tbsp cold water and mix for 20 to 30 seconds, or until the dough just binds together. You may need to add a little more water, but don't be too generous or the dough will become sticky. Wrap the dough in cling film and chill while making the pie filling.

Scoop out the seeds of a 1½ lb (750 g) wedge of pumpkin with a spoon. Or, if using a small pumpkin, cut in half and remove seeds. Cut pumpkin into small wedges and then cut into regular-sized slices for even cooking.

Using a dessertspoon, scoop the pumpkin flesh into the processor bowl and process to a smooth golden purée. Or purée in small batches in a liquidizer.

Spoon pumpkin purée into a bowl and stir in ½ pt (300 ml) milk, 2 eggs, 6 tbsp maple syrup, 3 tbsp plain flour, 1 tsp ground cinnamon, ¼ tsp freshly grated nutmeg, ¼ tsp ground ginger and a pinch of salt and mix until smooth. Set aside.

Ease the pastry into the base of the pie plate and press on to the sides with the fingertips. Trim pastry even with the pie plate.

Gently knead pastry trimmings and remaining one third of pastry together and roll out thinly. Cut leaf shapes and mark veins with a knife. Brush pastry edge with a little beaten egg and arrange leaves attractively on edge so that they overlap.

Pour the pumpkin mixture into the pastry case and place the pie on a baking sheet. Brush the pastry leaf edging with a little beaten egg and cook at Gas mark 6, 400°F, 200°C for 40 min.

Test the pumpkin pie by inserting a knife into the centre of the filling. If the knife comes out clean and the pastry is golden, then the pie is cooked. Arrange cooked maple leaves in the centre of the pie and serve it warm, cut into slices, with clotted cream.

Brian Turner's Chestnut Charlotte

Brian Turner describes his idea of glorious eating – beautifully presented dishes made of the best, freshest ingredients, tasting wonderful and looking like pictures on the plates – and it is difficult to imagine his very early years helping in his father's transport café in Yorkshire. Yet, he explains that the super-smart clientele at his new restaurant, Turner's, in London's Chelsea, are no more demanding. 'You can't serve rubbish to lorry drivers or anyone else!' Brian Turner trained in Leeds, worked at the Savoy and first became a talked-about chef in his days at the Capital Hotel in Knightsbridge. Now he has achieved 'every chef's dream, to be on my own'. In his Walton Street restaurant you'll see him in his trademark clogs, checking details.

'Of course, Christmas day itself is for traditional food, whole families get together round the table. But by the next day I want to get back to much lighter eating! The dessert given here is a new twist to the classic charlotte, perfect for a family gathering or sophisticated dinner party.'

'A creamy smooth chestnut and rum mousse encircled with sponge finger biscuits is just perfect for Christmas'

Brian has given two versions, but suggests that though the large one is impressive for a buffet, individual desserts are always the chef's choice for dinner. 'It's so much easier to make as there's no tricky slicing. The puddings can be kept in their moulds till needed, and can be successfully made the day before and chilled overnight. But don't serve them fridge-cold – leave at room temperature for an hour before serving so you can really taste the subtle flavours.

'I'm not going to say you must not use bought sponge fingers as a short cut, but with practice you'll master the art of making them. Fold in egg white and flour carefully, pipe evenly and bake as soon as you've finished a sheet or the mixture will "fall". When cooked, remove from the paper as soon as fingers are firm. The secret when lining a charlotte tin or mould is to butter the tin liberally and chill before using. That way, the fingers will stick to the tin.

'For a true charlotte the sponge fingers are always placed inside the mould before the filling, although I know some people add the fingers afterwards, once the mould is turned out. This isn't so good as the biscuits are too crisp in contrast to the melt-in-the-mouth filling.

'The pool of sauce in which the little puddings sit is an essential part of the recipe and it offsets the richness of the chestnut Bavarois. I like to pipe a little chestnut purée around the edge of the sauce and finish with a few pieces of marrons glacés, or tie a ribbon round a large charlotte. Remember, cooking is an art, so food should always look inviting.'

SERVES 10–12
INGREDIENTS:

FOR THE SPONGE FINGER BISCUITS:
4 eggs, separated
3½ oz (85 g) caster sugar
3½ oz (85 g) plain flour
few drops of vanilla essence

FOR THE MARRON BAVAROIS:
2 eggs, separated
4 oz (100 g) caster sugar
½ pt (300 ml) milk
4 teaspoons powdered gelatine
8 oz (250 g) can sweetened chestnut purée
2 tablespoons rum
½ pt (300 ml) double cream
4 pieces marrons glacés

FOR THE CRÈME ANGLAISE:
2 egg yolks
1 oz (25 g) caster sugar
¼ pt (150 ml) single cream
¼ pt (150 ml) milk
few drops of vanilla essence
1 tablespoon rum

TO DECORATE:
4 oz (100 g) couverture chocolate or cake covering
icing sugar to dust
1 small tube or 3 tablespoons sweetened chestnut purée
2 tablespoons rum
2 pieces marrons glacés, chopped

To make sponge fingers, place 4 egg yolks in a large bowl with 2 oz (50 g) caster sugar. Whisk until the mixture is very thick and creamy and leaves a trail when whisk is lifted.

Butter 12 dariole moulds or a deep 7 in (18 cm) charlotte tin; line bases with buttered greaseproof paper. Arrange cold biscuits side by side in large tin, top side outwards. For small puddings, trim biscuits to height of dariole moulds, trimmed ends to top.

Add 8 oz (250 g) chestnut purée and 2 tbsp rum to custard and whisk until smooth. Stand bowl in ice and chill, stirring occasionally until custard is very thick and just on the point of setting.

To make crème anglaise, whisk 2 egg yolks with 1 oz (25 g) caster sugar. Heat ¼ pt (150 ml) single cream and ¼ pt (150 ml) milk. Pour on to yolk mixture. Cook, see step 5, stirring until the custard coats the back of a wooden spoon. Cool.

2

Whisk 4 egg whites until stiff. Whisk in remaining 1½oz (35g) caster sugar, a spoon at a time, until smooth and glossy. Fold into yolk mixture alternately with 3½oz (85g) sifted plain flour, adding one third of each at a time. Fold in vanilla essence.

3

Spoon mixture into piping bag with a ¼in (5mm) tube. Pipe fingers 3in (7cm) long and well spaced on baking sheets lined with nonstick paper. Cook at Gas mark 4, 350°F, 180°C for 8 to 10min until pale golden. Cool and when firm, peel off paper.

5

To make bavarois, whisk 2 egg yolks and 2oz (50g) caster sugar until thick and creamy. Bring ½pt (300ml) milk to the boil. Pour on to yolk mixture steadily whisking. Return to the pan and heat gently, whisking lightly until custard coats the spoon. Don't boil.

6

Sprinkle 4tsp powdered gelatine over 3tbsp water, making sure that gelatine completely absorbs the water. Leave to soak for 5min. Add gelatine to hot custard and stir until dissolved. Cool custard, stirring occasionally so that a skin does not form.

8

Whip ½pt (300ml) double cream until just holding its shape. Whisk 2 egg whites until stiff, then whisk in 2oz (50g) caster sugar, a spoon at a time, until smooth and glossy. Fold cream, then egg whites into the custard. Chill until almost setting.

9

Spoon mixture into prepared tins so that they are half filled. Slice 4 pieces of marrons glacés and arrange on bavarois. Carefully spoon remaining mixture over to fill the tins. Chill for several hours or overnight until completely set.

11

To make curls, draw a vegetable peeler across a 4oz (100g) bar of chocolate or cake covering. Chill. Loosen mould and invert. Hold a cloth wrung out in hot water on base of tin for 1min and jerk plate. Remove tin. Dust curls with icing sugar; arrange.

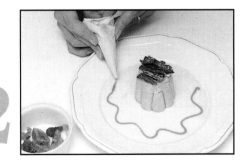

12

Stir vanilla essence and 1tbsp rum into crème anglaise. Spoon around individual charlottes. Beat 1 small tube or 3tbsp chestnut purée with 2tbsp rum. Pipe around sauce. Decorate with marrons glacés. Serve large charlotte and sauce separately.

Mary Norwak's Sparkling Lemon Grape Jelly

'If you thought jelly meant nursery fare, wait until you try this. It's clean, bright and wonderfully refreshing,' enthuses Mary Norwak. 'I find people really don't want to eat rich things in hot weather. Lemon jelly is just perfect for entertaining. A beautiful crystal clear jelly shimmering on a pretty glass plate is really the lightest, freshest way to finish a relaxed meal. I love it when all the family are home and we set out the food on a trestle table in the garden so that everyone can help themselves.'

Mary's family are grown up now, but she loves it when Sophie, Unity and son Matthew come home for the weekend. Mary became interested in cookery writing when her family was young and she first moved to Norfolk. Since then she has written more than 80 books about country cooking and enjoys researching Old English recipes.

'A sparkling jelly is really not difficult to make. The secret is to use scrupulously clean equipment – scald it with boiling water so there are no traces of grease. Use cube sugar in the recipe as it produces less scum than

'Refreshingly tangy with a fruity sweetness'

caster sugar or granulated sugar. Some people think that gelatine is tricky to use, but there's really no mystique. Just sprinkle the powdered gelatine over sufficient water to absorb every granule instantly and then leave for 5 minutes to soak or 'sponge'. Soaking this way helps to ensure every grain is dissolved when it's mixed into a quantity of liquid.

'To make the jelly really clear, bring it to the boil several times with a mixture of crushed eggshells and lightly whisked whites. The egg white and eggshells attract and soak up all the impurities that would otherwise make the jelly cloudy. As the mixture boils so the egg white and shells rise to the surface and form a thick white crust which acts as a filter and helps clarify the syrup. Pour the mixture into one of those old-fashioned jelly bags, the sort you use for jellied preserves (if you have difficulty obtaining one, a metal sieve lined with muslin will do instead). Leave the liquid to drip through slowly until it is completely clear.

'I much prefer to use a metal mould – the jellies turn out so much more easily than from ceramic ones. Choose one with good flutes so the pattern is well defined. Set the jelly in thin layers, otherwise the fruit floats to the top.

'To turn the jelly out, dip the mould up to the rim in hot water for 10 seconds. Invert the mould on to a serving plate, hold dish and mould together tightly with both hands and give a gentle shake. If the jelly proves stubborn, place a hot clean dishcloth on top of the mould and the jelly will slip out. A good trick when turning a mould out is to wet the serving plate, then you can gently tilt it and slide the dessert into position.

'There's something about a citrus jelly that is hard to beat. Experiment with different fruits in the layers – be creative and let your imagination take over.'

SERVES 6
INGREDIENTS:

1¾ oz (45 g) gelatine
3 lemons
7 oz (200 g) cube sugar
2 in (5 cm) piece of cinnamon stick
2 eggs
5 tablespoons dry sherry
8 oz (250 g) white muscat grapes
lemon geranium leaves and a few summer flowers to decorate

Place ½pt (250 ml) water in a bowl and sprinkle 1¾ oz (45 g) gelatine over. Leave for 5 min until the gelatine is completely absorbed by the water. Meanwhile, scald a large saucepan and a whisk, by rinsing with boiling water.

Separate 2 eggs and reserve the eggshells (you won't need to use the yolks in this recipe). Whisk the egg whites to a soft foam. Roughly crush the eggshells and add to the saucepan with the whisked whites and 5 tbsp dry sherry.

A thick white crust or 'filter' will have formed on top of the liquid. If the liquid beneath the crust is clear, carry on to the next stage; if it is still cloudy, bring to the boil one more time. Scald a thick jelly bag by pouring boiling water through it.

Halve and deseed 8 oz (250 g) bunch white muscat grapes and add to the remaining jelly. Leave at room temperature until required.

Pare the rind of 3 lemons thinly with a zester or vegetable peeler and squeeze the juice to extract 7 fl oz (175 ml). Place in pan with 1 pt (500 ml) water, 7 oz (200 g) cube sugar and 2 in (5 cm) cinnamon stick. Heat gently, until sugar dissolves.

Add the soaked gelatine and heat gently, stirring occasionally, until the gelatine has dissolved and the liquid is clear.

Whisk the mixture until the liquid begins to simmer. Allow the liquid to rise in the pan, without boiling over, whisking very gently.

Remove the whisk. Take pan from the heat and let liquid settle for about 5 min. Bring the liquid to the boil twice more, without whisking. Allow to settle between each boiling.

Hang bag from a cupboard handle or over an upturned stool. Place a bowl under bag. Pour mixture through and let it drip. Don't stir or squeeze. Remove bowl, replace with another and rinse bag with boiling water. Repeat straining until clear.

Rinse a 2 pt (1 litre) jelly mould with water and pour a little jelly into the base to a depth of about ½ in (1 cm). Chill in the fridge until set, or speed chilling by freezing briefly, taking care not to leave it for more than 15 to 20 min or jelly will become icy.

Spoon a layer of grapes with a little liquid jelly over the set jelly layer, position decoratively. Chill until set. Add a ½ in (1 cm) layer of jelly and chill until set. Repeat layering, alternating grapes and jelly, until the mould is full. Leave to set overnight in the fridge.

Dip the mould into hot water and count to ten. Remove from water and loosen edge of jelly with the fingertips. Invert the mould on to a plate and give a sharp shake. Remove mould and decorate jelly (discard flowers when serving).

BAKING

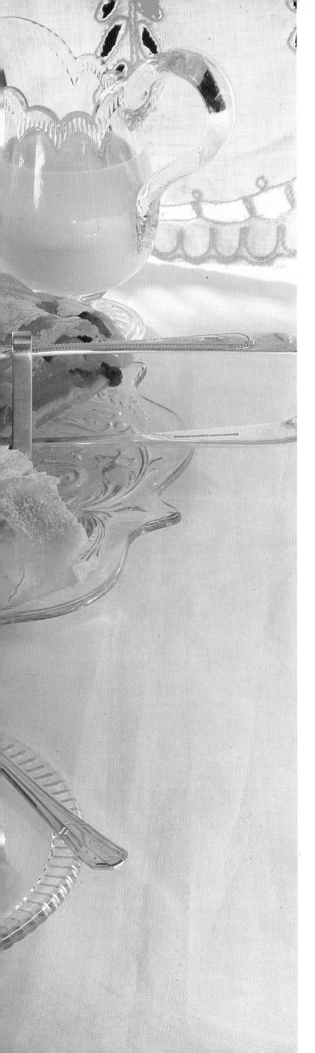

Rosemary Wadey's Apple Strudel

Mention Strudel and Rosemary Wadey instantly responds, 'Oh, I can taste it now, that delicious pastry melting in the mouth . . .' Strudel conjures up a cosy picture of a leisurely, mid-morning break, with fresh hot coffee accompanied by the warm apple strudel. It's equally popular as a dessert or teatime favourite. It was the Hungarians who first wrapped the incredibly thin strudel dough around an apple filling but the Viennese adopted *apfelstrudel* and it's now probably the most famous of their pastries.

Good strudel pastry is stretched so thinly that it ends up as thin as an onion skin. This quality for stretching is unusual in pastry, which has to be very short as a rule. Rosemary Wadey is a cookery writer who knows a lot about the many different types of pastry, methods and techniques for making it and a wide range of recipes.

'Strudel pastry is an exception to the general pastry-making formula,' she says. 'No light handling and keeping it cool – strudel pastry is kneaded like a bread dough, then left to relax, so it loses some of its springiness. I think perhaps the idea of making strudel pastry puts people off,

'Apple pie the Austrian way – layers of melt-in-the-mouth pastry with a spicy apple filling'

but it's really quite easy, and a lot of fun to do.

'Try to work quickly, especially when you have to "pull" the pastry out, and if the phone rings, *don't* go and answer it! The best thing about strudel pastry is that it breaks all the rules of pastry making. It's easier to make on a warm day, you can use warm water, warm the rolling pin, and warm hands are a bonus! Don't even worry if you've got long nails – just use clenched fists to pull the dough! Once you've made it for the first time you know your second attempt will be better, and the effort is so worthwhile. The finished pastry will keep in the freezer for up to three months. For Christmas strudel I add mincement, cranberries, or honey with dried apricots and nuts to the apple filling.'

Filo pastry is a very similar dough to strudel, made with strong plain flour and without eggs. If you're in a hurry, you can buy ready-rolled filo pastry.

In between eating strudels, Rosemary leads a 'desperately full life'. As a freelance home economist she is constantly asked to take on new assignments. She has just completed a new cake book and over the last eight years has written no less than 16 cookery books on a very wide range of subjects. She admits, 'It's lovely to be asked by publishers to write books and I thoroughly enjoy doing them. It's all go when I'm working on the book, then there's a long quiet gap after finishing before it appears in the shops. It's thrilling to see the work in print.'

Being freelance means that Rosemary's work is very varied. Many readers will know her as Cookery Editor of *Home and Country*, the Women's Institute publication.

Rosemary lives with her husband Andrew and their daughters Lucy and Laura in rural Sussex. Rosemary is very involved with the children and their main hobby – riding. 'They're horse mad,' she says. 'We've got five horses and the girls are crazy about the pony club, which I help to run. The girls compete in events and jumping. I love to join in whenever I'm not working; it gets me completely away from the kitchen, and helps to stop the pounds creeping on!'

MAKES 12 SLICES
INGREDIENTS:

FOR THE PASTRY:
8 oz (250 g) plain flour
good pinch of salt
1 beaten egg
2 tablespoons oil
FOR THE FILLING:
2 lb (1 kg) cooking apples
1½ oz (40 g) raisins
1½ oz (40 g) currants
3 oz (75 g) caster sugar
½ level teaspoon ground cinnamon or mixed spice
2½ oz (65 g) butter
4 oz (125 g) ground almonds
icing sugar to serve

To make the strudel pastry sift 8 oz (250 g) plain flour and a good pinch of salt into a bowl. Make a well in the centre and add 1 beaten egg, 2 tbsp oil and 4 tbsp warm water. Mix thoroughly to a soft, sticky, pliable dough.

Spread out 2 clean tea towels on the table, long selvedges together, and sprinkle with 1 to 2 tbsp flour. Place the dough in the centre and roll it out carefully, using a warmed rolling pin, to a rectangle about 18 × 12 in (45 × 30 in) and ⅛ in (3 mm) thick, lifting occasionally to prevent sticking.

Spoon the filling in a 3 in (7 cm) wide strip along shortest edge of the pastries, about 3 in (7 cm) from edge and leaving a margin at each end. Roll one pastry at a time: use both hands to lift the cloth and flip the edge of pastry over the filling. Turn in the ends of the dough along both long edges.

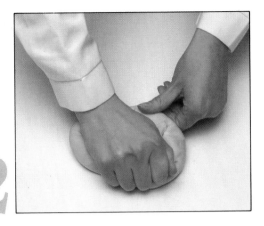

2 Turn the dough on to a floured surface and knead by hand for about 15 min, or in a large electric mixer fitted with a dough hook for about 5 min, until silky smooth and even. Shape the dough into a ball, place in an oiled polythene bag and leave to rest in a warm place for about 1 hour.

3 Meanwhile, prepare the filling: peel and core 2 lb (1 kg) cooking apples, and slice them very thinly. Combine with 1½ oz (40 g) each of raisins and currants, 3 oz (75 g) caster sugar and ½ level tsp ground cinnamon or mixed spice.

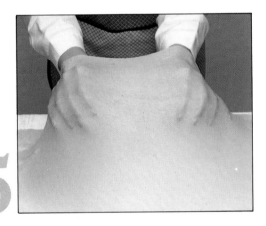

5 Now gently stretch the dough using the backs of the hands underneath it, and working from the centre outwards, until it is thin enough to read a newspaper through! Take care not to tear it. Stretch it to a rectangle 36 × 28 in (90 × 70 cm) so it entirely covers the 2 tea towels with thin pastry. Rest pastry for 15 min.

6 Trim off the thick edges of pastry overhanging the tea towels and discard. Melt 1½ oz (40 g) butter and brush it all over the surface of the pastry. Then cut the pastry in half between the 2 tea towels. Sprinkle evenly with 4 oz (125 g) ground almonds. Preheat oven to Gas mark 5, 375°F, 190°C.

8 Pull the cloth and the dough towards you and gently lift the cloth, a little at a time, to roll the dough on to itself. When it is completely rolled up, lift it, still in the cloth, on to a large, greased baking tray. Gently tip the dough on to the tray, at the same time positioning it so the 'seam' is underneath.

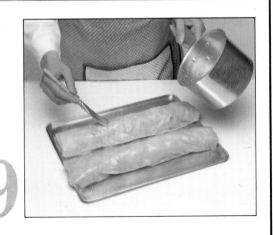

9 Roll up remaining strudel, and place beside the other on tray. Brush the tops with 1 oz (25 g) melted butter then bake just above centre of oven for about 30 min or until golden brown. Remove from baking tray using 2 fish slices. To serve: dust with icing sugar and serve in slices cut widthways, hot, warm or cold.

The Roux Brothers' Almond Meringue 'Japonais'

'I just love meringues – even as a child I could never refuse a meringue or a slice of a luscious meringue gâteau. I have such a sweet tooth – we both do – although my brother Albert knows when to say no, unlike me!' says Michel Roux. Michel and Albert Roux are renowned worldwide for their fabulous patisserie, a speciality in which they both served apprenticeships, and for which Michel has just been awarded the trophy for French Patisserie Personality of the Year.

'Brought up in the Saône-et-Loire district of France,' explains Michel, 'we were exposed to the finest traditions of French eating. Our mother was a superb cook and our father's *charcuterie* attracted a clientele from far and wide. We studied catering from the age of 14. We didn't attend college, but began working straight away, learning the basic skills as we went.

'We then both went into service with private households and embassies in France and England. Because of this background, when we opened Le Gavroche, our first restaurant, in London in 1967, our philosophy was to

'More sophisticated than plain meringue – almonds give a moist, chewy centre – it's irresistible'

provide the highest quality in cuisine and service. *All* our clients are VIPs: the fact they love good food classes them as gourmets in our eyes! Neither of us had ever run a restaurant before – or any other business. What we did have, though, was a lifetime's experience of working with good food – and a lot of determination.'

In 1982 theirs was the first restaurant in Britain to be awarded three stars in the Michelin guide – the highest accolade. They now have five restaurants; Michel runs The Waterside Inn at Bray, and Albert runs Le Gavroche.

'When I have been too busy in the restaurant to have lunch, I love to have afternoon tea,' sighs Michel. 'Our individual Almond Meringues 'Japonais' are perfect for tea time; the larger one makes a luscious dessert.

'The secret when making the meringue is to whisk the egg whites in a large grease-free bowl. Start by whisking the egg whites slowly to make them frothy and stretch them as much as possible, then increase the speed to firm them up and incorporate the maximum amount of air. When they are softly peaking, fold in the sugar, then continue whisking until firm but not dry. If you over-whisk them you will find it difficult to fold in the almond mixture. Sprinkle it over the egg whites and fold in with a slotted spoon. It should take only two or three minutes.

'Keep an eye on the meringues while they are cooking – turn the temperature down and cook for a little longer if they are browning too quickly. If you cannot peel away the nonstick baking paper, return the meringues to the turned-off oven, leaving them to complete cooking in the residual heat.

'When entertaining, make the meringue layers up to ten days in advance and store in an airtight tin, interleaved with nonstick paper. Then simply make the crème pâtissière on the day and assemble just before serving.'

SERVES 6
INGREDIENTS:

4½ oz (125 g) ground almonds
4½ oz (125 g) icing sugar
6 egg whites, size 2
1 oz (25 g) caster sugar
½ oz (15 g) plain flour
1 oz (25 g) flaked almonds, chopped
FOR THE CRÈME PÂTISSIÈRE FILLING:
6 egg yolks
4½ oz (125 g) caster sugar
1½ oz (40 g) plain flour
18 fl oz (500 ml) milk
1 vanilla pod
TO DECORATE:
icing sugar, for dusting
selection of summer fruits
(red and white currants, raspberries, strawberries)
coulis of raspberries made from 1 lb (500 g) fruit, puréed, sieved and lightly sweetened

Line 3 baking sheets with nonstick baking paper. Either draw 24, 2 in (5 cm) circles using a pastry cutter as a guide (leave plenty of space between the circles). Or, draw three 8 in (20 cm) circles using a plate as a guide. Turn paper over before piping.

Scatter one third of the almond and icing sugar mixture and ½ oz (15 g) sifted plain flour over the egg whites. Fold in gently with a slotted spoon. Add the remaining mixture in two batches – stop folding in as soon as they are well mixed. Do not overwork.

Sprinkle over 1 oz (25 g) chopped flaked almonds. Cook at Gas mark 2, 300°F, 150°C for 40 min for the small circles and 1 hour for the large. Check after 20 min and rearrange baking sheets. When cooked, turn over and peel away paper carefully.

Pour the egg mixture into the rest of the milk in the saucepan and bring slowly to the boil, stirring. Boil for 2 min, stirring continuously until thick. Pour into a bowl to cool.

Sift 4½ oz (125 g) finely ground almonds and 4½ oz (125 g) icing sugar into a bowl. Stir until evenly mixed and reserve.

Place 6 egg whites in a large grease-free bowl and whisk until softly peaking. Whisk in 1 oz (25 g) caster sugar and continue whisking until the mixture is firm but not dry.

If making the small circles, spoon the meringue mixture into a large piping bag fitted with a ¼ in (5 mm) plain piping nozzle. Starting from the centre of the circle, pipe a tight spiral until you reach the edge. Continue piping until all the mixture is used up.

For the larger bases, spoon the almond meringue mixture into a piping bag fitted with a ½ in (1 cm) plain nozzle. Pipe three circles in the same way, working from the centre to the edge.

To make the crème pâtissière, place 6 egg yolks in a bowl with 1½ oz (40 g) caster sugar and whisk until they are pale and fall in a light ribbon from the beaters. Sift over 1½ oz (40 g) plain flour and continue whisking until smooth and glossy.

Place 18 fl oz (500 ml) milk in saucepan with 3 oz (85 g) caster sugar and vanilla pod. Bring almost to the boil, stirring occasionally until sugar dissolves. Remove vanilla pod. Gradually pour about one third on to the egg mixture, stirring until smooth.

Dust the surface of the crème pâtissière with just enough sifted icing sugar to cover surface lightly, but completely, to prevent a skin forming as it cools.

Spread the cooled crème pâtissière over one meringue circle to cover completely. Top with another circle, then make a third layer in the same way. Decorate with fruits in season and serve, if liked, with raspberry coulis.

Jennie Reekie's Bûche de Noël

Jennie Reekie spent six months researching information and testing recipes for a book on cooking with chocolate, and this classic French 'chocolate log' is one of her favourites. Chocoholics among us would find the prospect of such research very appealing – imagine being surrounded by chocolate cakes, desserts and fudges, day in and day out, becoming more friendly with the neighbours but more terrified of the bathroom scales! Jennie and her two teenage daughters (chief tasters) survived the experience, and admit that even though a diet of chocolate recipes begins to pall after a time, some chocolatey things are so good, they are always irresistible. Like, for instance, this dreamy chocolate log, based on a simple Swiss roll. It traditionally appears in French homes at Christmas and is known there as *Bûche de Noël*.

'At one time, people were afraid of whisked sponge mixtures,' says Jennie, 'because if the eggs and sugar weren't beaten for long enough the end result was more like a large biscuit than a light sponge. Whisked sponges do require a lot of beating – but nowadays electric whisks

'If you can resist eating this French classic straightaway, it'll freeze for several weeks!'

have taken the sweat out of beating the mixture, and they give really good results.

'The aim of whisking is to get a large volume of mixture and when you can do this simple test you're ready for the next stage: lift the whisk from the bowl, allowing the mixture to fall from the whisk leaving a trail. If the trail does not submerge, but sits on top of the mixture for about 15 seconds, it is ready for the next stage. It may take some time to reach this point, but then the cake is almost completed. Sift the flour and cocoa on top and fold it in carefully so you don't knock out all the air that you've conscientiously whisked in! Always sift the cocoa powder to get rid of all lumps.

'Cocoa gives a strong chocolate flavour, particularly good in baking, but not rich. I find this type of cake is best made with cocoa as the ones made with melted chocolate tend to crack. Provided you don't overcook this, it won't crack, and even if it does, don't be disappointed, because you're going to cover it all over with a chocolate cream anyway!

'A whisked sponge does not contain fat, so it is drier than a creamed cake. It lends itself to a very rich filling, but stales quickly and is best eaten on the day it is made. It also freezes well, so you can make it several weeks in advance. Open-freeze on a cake board and then wrap when frozen. I'm not a great "deep freezer", but you can always freeze just the Swiss roll, with the greaseproof paper rolled up inside, then thaw and fill when required.

'It's the filling of this cake that makes it so special. It will appeal to those who do not have a sweet tooth, because it has a creamy custard base, chocolate of course, mixed with a light, smooth butter cream.'

Despite all this talk of chocolate Jennie has plenty of variety in her work – she has been a freelance home economist for years, and writing, public relations, preparing food for advertising photographs and TV commercials take up most of her time.

INGREDIENTS:

4 eggs
4 oz (125 g) caster sugar
3 oz (75 oz) self-raising flour
1 oz (25 g) cocoa powder
¼ pt (150 ml) milk
2 egg yolks
6 oz (175 g) plain dark chocolate
4 oz (125 g) unsalted butter
2 oz (50 g) icing sugar, plus a little extra
TO DECORATE:
Christmas cake decorations

Prepare a hot oven (Gas mark 6, 400°F, 200°C). Grease a 13 × 9 in (33 × 23 cm) Swiss roll tin and place on a piece of greaseproof paper 15 × 12 in (38 × 30 cm). Mark corners and fold in edges. Snip paper at corners, ease into tin and grease.

Turn the mixture into the prepared tin, but don't be tempted to smooth surface – just tip the tin so that the mixture flows into corners. Tap tin on work surface once. Bake in a hot oven for 12 to 15 min until the cake springs back when pressed lightly.

To make the filling, heat ¼ pt (150 ml) milk to blood temperature (until it feels neither hot nor cold when tested with your finger) in a small saucepan. Blend 2 egg yolks in a heatproof basin or the top of a double saucepan, and beat in the milk.

Cream 4 oz (125 g) unsalted butter and beat in 2 oz (50 g) icing sugar, sifted, then gradually beat in the cooled chocolate custard. Unroll the Swiss roll, and spread with one third of the filling. Do not chill filling before use, as it won't soften again for spreading.

Whisk 4 eggs and 4oz (125g) caster sugar together until thick and creamy. Use an electric mixer or use a hand-held mixer and a large bowl over a pan of hot water. The mixture is ready when it leaves a trail for 15 seconds after lifting out the whisk.

Sift in 3oz (75g) self-raising flour and 1oz (25g) cocoa powder. Fold into the mixture very carefully, using a large metal spoon or plastic spatula, by cutting through mixture, lifting it from base of bowl, and shaking flour and cocoa back into egg mixture.

Turn out on to a piece of greaseproof or nonstick silicone paper dredged with caster sugar. Carefully peel off the lining paper. Trim off the crisp edges, as they would crack as you roll. Cut a line 1in (2.5cm) in from a short edge, but don't slice through.

Fold indented end over to start a neat roll. Then roll up the cake, keeping the paper inside and working away from you. Roll gently but firmly to prevent cracking. Put the roll on one side and allow to cool.

Stand the basin over a pan of gently simmering water, and cook, stirring frequently, until the mixture coats the back of a wooden spoon and a finger drawn through the mixture on the spoon leaves a clear path. This will take about 15min.

Add 6oz (175g) plain dark chocolate broken into small pieces, and stir until it has melted, then remove basin from the heat. Cover the basin with a piece of clingfilm and leave until cool, stirring from time to time. Do not refrigerate.

Re-roll carefully and quite loosely – without the paper – so the filling doesn't ooze out. Transfer to serving dish or cake board at this stage if you like. Spread the outside of the roll with the remaining chocolate cream, and cover ends, too.

Using a fork, make lines on the top of the log, as if for the bark of a tree. Chill in a refrigerator for about 1 hour until set, then sift ½tsp icing sugar over. Decorate with appropriate cake decorations before serving.

Lizzie Boyd's Danish Pastries

When Lizzie Boyd first came here from her native Denmark, she looked in vain for Danish pastries. After the austere 1950s, things began to change, though, and Lizzie, editor of many bestselling cookbooks, has been watching with well-informed interest as many Continental delicacies have gradually become available all over the country. But, she explains, the so-called Danish pastries sold here are not the real thing.

'Just as other nationalities don't understand the British pub, the British have never understood what a real Danish pastry is like. It should be a soft pastry with a yielding quality, a soft filling and a crisp sugar topping. It should be eaten while still warm from the oven. In Denmark you can buy these wherever the "Vienna Baker" sign is displayed. Otherwise, you just have to be like me and make them at home! I prepare the dough the night before and sometimes even shape all the pastries, leave them in the fridge, then bring them back to room temperature before glazing and baking for my guests.

'It's funny that something the world thinks of as Danish

'Just like biting into soft layers of buttery air, filled with delicious scents and tastes'

isn't at all. Our name for them is *Wienerbrød*, which means Vienna breads. Bakers from Vienna settled in Denmark after the First World War and they brought this recipe with them.

'For Danes, our Vienna breads are a treat for special occasions, something to enjoy when you go to a café for coffee or tea, and what you have when you've been working very hard. My mother used to send me out for them during the enormous, once a month household wash. I'd take the orders; so many wanted "cockscombs", so many wanted "snails". My favourite was always a round "cremebolle" which I had each birthday. The variations are endless and though I've given just the traditional Danish "remonte" filling you could make up a puréed apple and sultana filling or use pastry cream.

'Today, I make Danish pastries whenever I have special guests or a special occasion, like Easter Sunday tea. You have to start well in advance as the dough needs to be chilled well before rolling and folding. I like to chill the rolling pin, too. You'll find it helps to roll it when it is still cool but just soft enough to leave the impression of a finger.

'Life is much easier now we can use easy-blend dried yeast, which doesn't have to be frothed up first and, once you've made the dough, I think you'll find the shaping is pure fun. Do try Danish pastries warm from the oven and don't dream of giving them up for Lent but follow the Danish tradition and decorate your "cremeboller" with white glacé icing rather than chocolate during that time.'

MAKES 24
INGREDIENTS:

1 lb 2 oz (500 g) plain flour
2 tablespoons caster sugar
pinch of salt
2 oz (50 g) lard
2 sachets easy-blend dried yeast
1 egg
8 fl oz (250 ml) milk
8 oz (250 g) butter
FOR THE REMONTE FILLING:
4 oz (125 g) butter
4 oz (125 g) caster sugar
4 oz (125 g) ground almonds
1 egg, beaten, to glaze
TOPPINGS:
2 teaspoons ground cinnamon
1 teaspoon strawberry jam
2 tablespoons flaked almonds
3 tablespoons caster sugar
7 tablespoons icing sugar
1 teaspoon cocoa powder
little grated chocolate

Sift 1 lb 2 oz (500 g) plain flour, 2 tbsp caster sugar and a pinch of salt. Rub in 2 oz (50 g) lard until mixture resembles fine crumbs. Stir in 2 sachets easy-blend dried yeast. Lightly beat 1 egg with 8 fl oz (250 ml) milk, pour in and mix to a soft dough.

Place dough on floured surface so top overlap is on your left. Roll out to same size as before with light even strokes. Cover and chill 10 min. Repeat twice more. If butter is 'streaking'. chill for 30 min between rollings and roll between greaseproof paper.

To make 'snails', spread a little remonte filling over remaining two strips to cover, leaving a thin border of dough. Sprinkle with 1 tsp ground cinnamon. Roll up each strip, starting with one long edge. Brush edge with egg and place join underneath.

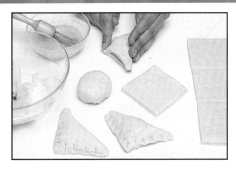

Spoon filling in centre of 8 squares. Brush edges with egg. To make four 'triangles' fold in half diagonally, seal. Make small cuts in short edges. To make four 'cremeboller', gather edges to make rounds, join underneath. Brush with egg; leave to rise.

2 Knead dough until shiny and smooth. Wrap in oiled clingfilm and chill. Roll out evenly 8oz (250g) butter at room temperature between two sheets of greaseproof paper until 15 × 4 in (38 × 10 cm). Chill in freezer for 10 min.

3 Knead dough again and roll out 2 in (5 cm) larger than butter. Peel away one paper from butter, turn over and place on dough. Peel away top paper. Fold top third of dough to centre. Fold bottom third over to cover. Chill in oiled clingfilm for 10 min.

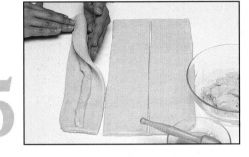

5 Roll half of dough to 9 × 12 in (23 × 30 cm). Cut into three. Make filling by creaming butter with caster sugar. Stir in almonds. To make 'cockscombs', place a thin rope of remonte along centre of one strip. Brush edges with egg, fold over, seal.

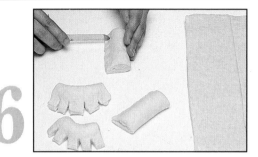

6 Cut the filled strip into four even-sized pieces. Make four cuts along sealed edges almost through to filling. Curve edge to open out cuts. Place on baking sheet lined with foil. Brush with egg and leave in a warm place for 15 min or until well risen.

8 Cut both strips into four even pieces. Make one cut almost to the filling in the centre of each piece. Curve four to open out cuts. To shape rest, hold each end and twist gently in opposite directions. Place on the baking sheet, brush with egg and leave to rise.

9 Roll out remaining dough as before. Cut into 12 3in (7 cm) squares. Brush four with egg. To make each 'spandau', bring two corners to centre, seal. Turn and repeat. Place a ball of filling in centre and top with jam. Brush with egg and leave to rise.

11 Reglaze with egg. Sprinkle 2 tbsp almonds over 'triangles', 1 tbsp caster sugar over 'cockscombs', 1 tsp cinnamon and 2 tbsp caster sugar over 'snails'. Cook at Gas mark 6, 400°F, 200°C for 8 min, then Gas mark 4, 350°F, 180°C for 5 to 8 min.

12 Mix 4 tbsp sifted icing sugar with 2 tsp water to a paste and pipe zig-zags over each 'snail' and 'spandau'. Sift 3 tbsp icing sugar and 1 tsp cocoa, stir in 2 tsp water to a smooth paste, spoon over 'cremeboller', and sprinkle with chocolate.

Elizabeth David's Hot Cross Buns

'Discover the joy of home-baked hot cross buns, well spiced and fresh from the oven: they're entirely delicious,' says renowned cookery writer Elizabeth David enthusiastically. 'These plump, soft, sweet fermented cakes are an English institution, but one of those specialities that are seldom made at home.

'Many people shy away from the thought of baking with yeast, yet it is immensely satisfying and there really is no mystery attached: the secret is to keep everything warm so that the yeast rapidly multiplies, raising the dough. Cream the yeast with a little tepid milk and the minute it comes into contact with the warm liquid it starts coming back to life. There is no need to add sugar at this stage as modern baker's yeast does not need it; it's a myth that fresh yeast needs sugar as "food". As soon as the yeast is added to warmed flour it will start its job of converting flour starch into its own form of sugar. Yeast freezes well for up to 3 months. Cut into handy 1oz (30g) pieces, wrap with clingfilm and polybag. Thaw at room temperature.

'Part of the charm of hot cross buns is their lovely

'The aroma of home-baked hot cross buns is irresistibly enticing'

brownish crumb, which is a result of flavouring with soft brown sugar and mixed sweet spices. Making up your own spice blend gives the best flavour; I've worked out the following mixture and use it frequently for spicing currant loaves and cakes as well as hot cross buns, of course. It's 1 large nutmeg, 3 teaspoons white peppercorns or allspice berries, a 6 inch (15 cm) cinnamon stick, 2 teaspoons of cloves and a 2 inch (5 cm) piece of dried root ginger. I grind all this in my very ancient coffee mill – although not as fine as commercially ground spice; I much prefer it a little coarser. Store whatever you don't use, but only up to six months as spices stale quickly – remember to date the jar. I like to mix a little ground cumin into the dough, too. Although unorthodox, its wonderfully warm and attractive flavour is well worth trying – but don't add any leftovers to your spice jar, as cumin quickly loses its aroma.

'I've found the easiest and quickest way to shape the buns is just to spoon the dough into lightly greased sections of a tartlet tray. As they rise they become well rounded.

'The dough for hot cross buns should be slightly firmer than for other bun doughs, so it will take the cross cuts without losing shape during cooking. Make the cuts fairly deeply with the back of a knife or thin metal spatula. To emphasize the cross, some bakers superimpose strips of candied peel or little bands of ordinary pastry. Both these methods involve unnecessary fiddly work, and neither, in my experience, is successful. There's no need to worry over-much about the exactness of the cross. You've made the symbolic gesture, that's what counts.'

MAKES 20
INGREDIENTS:

½ pt (300 ml) milk
1 oz (30 g) fresh baker's yeast
1 lb 2 oz (500 g) strong plain flour
1 teaspoon salt
2 teaspoons mixed sweet spices
2 oz (60 g) soft light brown sugar
2 oz (60 g) softened butter
2 eggs
4 oz (125 g) currants
2 tablespoons caster sugar

Measure ½ pt (300 ml) milk and reserve 2 tbsp for the glaze. Warm remaining milk to blood heat, until it feels just tepid. Cream 1 oz (30 g) fresh yeast with a little of the milk. Place 1 lb 2 oz (500 g) strong plain flour, 1 tsp salt, 2 tsp mixed sweet spices and 2 oz (60 g) soft light brown sugar in a large warmed bowl. Stir well.

Cover the bowl with clingfilm and leave the dough to rise in a warm place for 1 to 2 hours or until it is at least double in volume, light and puffy.

Make a deep cross cut in each bun with the back of a knife. The buns will flatten slightly on cutting, but will rise to a lovely rounded shape again on cooking. Leave for 10 min until cuts have just opened out.

2 Make a well in the centre of the bowl. Add 2oz (60g) softened butter, pour in the yeast. Stir in 2 eggs, one at a time, and the rest of the milk, or as much of it as can be absorbed by the dough, which should be soft but not sticky. Mix with a wooden spoon or by hand until smooth.

3 Add 4oz (125g) currants and mix well with a wooden spoon or by hand until evenly distributed.

5 Now break down the dough – turn out on to a lightly floured surface and give it a good punch with your fist. Gather it up, folding it over on itself in a roughly three-cornered fashion and punch again. Continue for 3 or 4min to redistribute yeast bubbles.

6 Using a tablespoon, break off spoonfuls of dough and fill 20 lightly greased sections of tartlet tins. Dome up the dough for a good plump shape, smooth surface with a palette knife. Cover with lightly oiled clingfilm and leave for about 15min until the buns have recovered volume, are well rounded and almost touching.

8 Bake in a preheated oven Gas mark 6, 400°F, 200°C for 15 to 20min until well rounded and golden brown. Check by tapping base of bun: it should sound hollow when cooked.

9 Just before the buns are ready to come out of the oven, make a glaze by boiling the reserved 2tbsp milk and 2tbsp caster sugar in a small saucepan until bubbling and syrupy. Brush the buns with the glaze while they are still hot to give them a fine, shining, mirror-like finish.

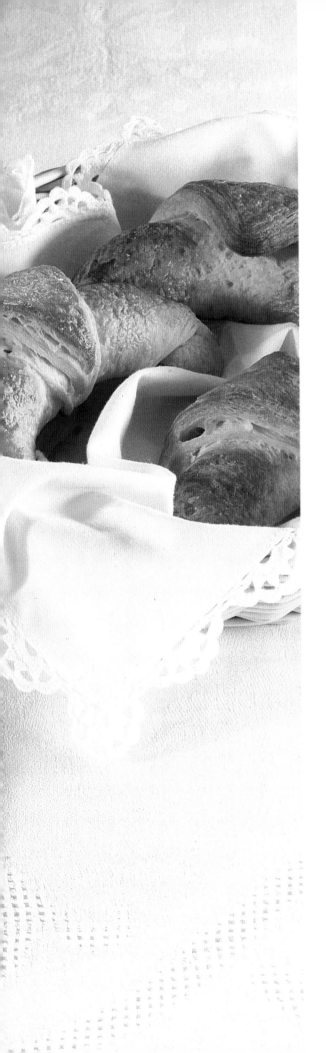

Glynn Christian's Croissants

What better way to start the day than eating a flaky, buttery croissant, watching one of Glynn Christian's *Breakfast Time* spots and knowing that you've just successfully made one of the trickiest but most satisfying doughs? Glynn himself has learned how to make croissants by trial and error.

He is the great, great, great, great grandson of Fletcher Christian, leader of the 1789 mutiny on the *Bounty*, and the founder of the Pitcairn Islands. Also a great traveller, Glynn claims that his knowledge of food has been gathered from all corners of the world. He was born in New Zealand, and has lived in Britain since 1965. He opened his own delicatessen several years ago, before turning to journalism and broadcasting.

He doesn't believe recipes to be exact formulas, but more an interesting read, inviting the reaction: 'Gosh, I never knew that!' He has a natural enthusiasm for food, and this 'gosh' factor bubbles over into his recipes.

There's no better way to learn about food than by comparison, and that's how Glynn learned to make

'Croissants are one of the heights of yeast baking made by rolling up a rich, yeasted dough with layers of a great deal of butter'

CROISSANTS

croissants: 'When I first opened my delicatessen ten years ago I was lucky to sell even six croissants a week. Two years later I was selling nearly 50 dozen. But as the number crept up, the quality declined. By experimenting in my own kitchen I was able to advise my baker where he was going wrong. However, it wasn't until I was filming in Venice for *Pebble Mill At One* that I saw the chefs preparing croissants for the following morning and really learned how to shape them properly. I keep discovering new tips even now. Croissants are found throughout Europe, varying mainly in their sweetness. Polish and Austrian are the sweetest. Several places claim the invention of these crescents of cholesterol – I plump for the Viennese baker who is said to have fashioned them on the morning the "crescents" on the flags of the invading Turks were finally repelled from his city gates!

'Making croissants is neither easy nor quick, but if you fit it into your routine, the time you actually spend is not that great. With experience you will get the feel of the dough. Always give it plenty of time to rise. Where you leave the dough to rise depends on the type of day: on a hot day, sit the bowl of dough on a sunny windowsill, where it will thrive, otherwise put it in a nice warm kitchen or airing cupboard. A hot steamy bathroom is another possibility.

'Always allow plenty of time to chill the dough, too, and don't worry if you have to go out during the day – it will be all the better for chilling in the fridge. When rolling out the croissants, work in a cool kitchen – open all the windows and doors if necessary or you will find the buttery layers melting. Don't expect your croissants to come out like the commercial ones. What's the point in making something exactly like the ones you can so easily buy? If you've gone to all the trouble of making them you certainly want your family or friends to know, and "taste" the difference. They might not always turn out perfectly shaped but they will be reliably wicked, buttery and delicious.'

MAKES 8
INGREDIENTS:

1 oz (25 g) fresh yeast or
½ oz (15 g) dried yeast with a pinch of sugar
¼ pt (150 ml) lukewarm, scalded milk (see step 1)
1 oz (25 g) butter or lard
1 teaspoon salt
1 tablespoon sugar
12 oz (375 g) strong white flour
4 oz (125 g) butter, chilled
egg and milk for glaze

1 Stir fresh yeast or dried yeast and sugar into 3 tbsp warm water. Heat milk to just below boiling point, pour into mixing bowl and cool until lukewarm. Melt with butter or lard, salt and sugar; add to the milk. Add yeast and stir well.

4 Leave the dough to rise until doubled in size and a dent remains after prodding. Set the bowl in a suitable place, ensuring that the warmth surrounds it evenly and does not come from just one angle.

7 Fold one third of the dough into the centre then fold the other third over that. This begins the layering of butter between the dough. The more the dough is rolled and folded the flakier the end result will be.

10 Cut the dough in half. Roll out each half into an even square and cut into 4 triangle shapes with a base of about 6 in (15 cm). Always use a razor-sharp knife, and never drag or press the dough as this will compress the layers.

2

Work in 12 oz (375 g) strong white flour. Mix in with a wooden spoon and when all the flour is incorporated, gather the dough together with your hands and turn on to a lightly floured work surface.

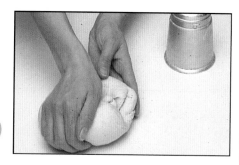

3

Knead thoroughly: fold the dough in half, pushing the heel of the palm down through the dough. Rock it back again and turn through a quarter circle. Continue until really smooth and supple. Place in a lightly oiled bowl, cover with clingfilm.

5

Remove the risen dough from the bowl to 'knock' or 'punch' it down. This is done to redistribute the gas bubbles formed by the growth of the yeast. Punch the dough once, firmly in the middle. Knead lightly, cover, and chill thoroughly.

6

Roll out the dough on a floured work surface to a strip three times longer than it is wide. Dot 4 oz (125 g) well-chilled butter in even rows all over the dough.

8

Seal the edges with a rolling pin, and press down lightly on the centre. This prevents butter escaping when the dough is rolled out again and seals in some air. Give the dough a half turn and roll out to the original size (as in step 6). Chill for 10 to 15 min.

9

Fold the dough in three, seal, and roll out again. Chill for 10 to 15 min. Repeat the rolling and folding *at least twice more*. Cover with clingfilm and chill thoroughly in the fridge between each process. The dough can now be left in the fridge overnight.

11

Lightly roll the point of the triangle to elongate it, and pull the corners of the base apart a little. Then roll up from the base. Curve into a crescent shape and space out on an oiled baking sheet; cover lightly with oiled clingfilm.

12

Prove in a warm place for 20 to 30 min until doubled in size, then chill for 10 min. Brush with a mixture of lightly beaten egg and milk. Bake at Gas mark 7, 425°F, 220°C for 15 min until golden and crisp. Eat as soon as possible.

Jocasta Innes's Strawberry Jam

Jocasta Innes is a lady of many talents, and gets great satisfaction from learning something new and doing it properly. 'When I was very hard up, preserving food, especially using up gluts of seasonal fruit and vegetables, was a satisfying way of saving money. I found that I could make money this way too, simply by writing about what I was most interested in.' Her recipes combine the best of the old ways with a keen appreciation of the advantages of modern methods and gadgets. Her range covers baking, bottling, brewing, cheese-making, salting, smoking and drying foods as well as traditional jams, jellies and chutneys. The recipes are international too. Born in China, Jocasta has travelled widely. She is now married to novelist Joe Potts, living and working in London and caring for four children.

'I miss my country living sometimes – we used to live in Swanage and had a long garden and an allotment. There I grew everything and was able to gather wild fruit and vegetables to preserve.'

Even now, wherever she goes on holiday, she can be

'Good jam appeals to the artist in every cook; fine colour and brilliance count for almost as much as good flavour'

found collecting foods to preserve. 'It's a magical feeling to stand back and look at all those lovely glistening jars full of goodness. They look so perfect that it's a shame to open them. I'm very possessive of my preserves and find them even more rewarding now that I have less time to do them!

'Strawberry jam must be everyone's favourite preserve but before we begin making it, some methodology is helpful. The basic definition of a jam is: whole fruit or fruit pulp boiled with sugar till such time as the acid and pectin in the fruit combine with the thickening sugar syrup to make the mixture set or gel.

'Let us deal first with the pectin and acid question. Pectin is a gummy substance naturally found in some fruit more than others. Ditto for acid. Acid helps draw out the pectin during cooking. The pectin then combines with the sugar to produce a good gel or set, so it follows that fruit high in both is good for jam.

'Green cooking apples, blackcurrants, redcurrants, damsons, plums, gooseberries and quinces are all high in pectin and acid, so they gel or jam effortlessly. Fresh apricots, loganberries, raspberries, greengages and early blackberries have a medium pectin/acid content; strawberries have a low one.

'Slightly underripe fruit is at its peak for pectin/acid and this is the best to use. Testing fruit for pectin is easy and can be useful in deciding how much sugar to use (see step 4). A simple rule is that high pectin sets more sugar and so equals more jam. However, a more accurate version with measures is:

High pectin fruits
1¼–1½lb (575–675g) sugar to 1lb (450g) fruit.
Medium pectin fruits
1lb (450g) sugar to 1lb (450g) fruit.
Low pectin fruits
12oz (350g) sugar to 1lb (450g) fruit.

'Adding the juice of 1 lemon to each 1lb (450g) strawberries therefore extracts the maximum amount of pectin from the fruit, and 14oz (400g) sugar to 1lb (450g) strawberries should be sufficient to set the jam, which has a lovely fresh fruity flavour.' Granulated sugar is quite adequate, but preserving sugar gives a finer flavour.

MAKES ABOUT 6–7lb (2.75–3kg)
INGREDIENTS:
4lb (2kg) ripe, sound strawberries
4 lemons
3½lb (1.75kg) preserving or granulated sugar

Take 4lb (2kg) of ripe but sound fruit, pick over for stalks and leaves and remove hulls. The strawberries should not be washed, but should be wiped instead with a clean cloth.

To test for pectin, take 1tsp juices from the pre-cooked fruit and place on a saucer with 1tbsp methylated spirits. Swirl. If 1 jelly blob forms, the fruit mixture is rich in pectin. If 2 or 3 form, it is relatively well off. If smaller beads or none at all appear, you must add high-pectin fruit or commercial pectin.

Alternatively, drop a tiny bit of boiling jam on a clean saucer: allow to cool. Push with your fingertip or the handle of a teaspoon. If it wrinkles, the jam is done. Remove the pan from the heat while testing the set or it may over-cook. As soon as the jam is judged ready, remove the pan from the heat.

Put the prepared fruit into a preserving pan with the juice of 4 lemons. It needs to be a large pan, 1½–2 gallon (6–9 litre) capacity, shallow but wide to help evaporation, and solid to distribute heat and guard against sticking. This may seem very large, but it should never be more than half full.

Simmer the fruit over a low heat until the strawberries are quite soft and mushy, about 30 min. Measure 3½ lb (1.75 kg) sugar and warm in a low oven before adding. Wash and dry the jam jars thoroughly and place on a baking tray ready to be warmed in the oven when the sugar comes out.

Turn off the heat, add the warmed sugar to the softened fruit. Stir vigorously to dissolve, turn on the heat and bring quickly back to the boil. This jam takes approximately 15 min to reach a set.

A jam-making thermometer shows at a glance if the jam is ready to set. First it should always be warmed in a jug of hot water. It will soon read up to within a couple of degrees of setting point (105°C, 221°F), the last degree always taking the longest to reach.

Leave the jam to cool and set slightly for 20 min. Ladle into a jug, then pour through a jam funnel into the clean, warmed jars to within ¼ in (5 mm) of the rims. Wipe drips and any stickiness off the jars with a hot damp cloth. Leave to cool completely without disturbing it.

To keep well, all preserves should be given an airtight seal with the waxed paper discs sold in sizes to fit standard jars. The jar itself can be covered with cellophane, paper doilies, or rounds of check gingham. Polish the jars with a clean, dry cloth and label neatly with the name of the jam and the date.

INDEX

Acknowledgments

Photographs are by John Elliott, styling by Judy Williams, except where otherwise stated

8 – 11 Recipe from 'English Cookery New and Old' by Susan Campbell (The Consumers' Association and Hodder & Stoughton, £7.95); photographs by Julie Fisher

12 – 15 Recipe from 'The Complete Asian Cookbook' by Terry Tan (Marshall Cavendish, price £14.95)

16 – 19 Recipe from 'Cuisine Végétarienne Française' by Jean Conil with Fay Franklin (Thorsons, £9.95); stylist Carol Pastor

20 – 23 Recipe from 'The Miller Howe Cookbook' by John Tovey (Century Hutchinson, £14.95)

24 – 27 Recipe from 'Julia Child's Kitchen' by Julia Child (Jonathan Cape Ltd, £9.50)

28 – 31 Recipe from 'The Romantic Vegetarian' by Colin Spencer (Thorsons Publishing)

34 – 37 Recipe from 'Fish Cookery' by Jane Grigson (Penguin, £3.50)

38 – 41 Recipe from 'The Fish Course' by Susan Hicks (BBC Books, £6.95)

42 – 45 Recipe from 'Japanese Cookery' by Elisabeth Lambert Ortiz (Collins, £9.95)

46 – 49 Recipe from 'Floyd on Fish' by Keith Floyd (BBC, in association with Absolute Press, £3.95)

50 – 53 Recipe by Patricia Lousada from 'American Sampler' (Woodhead Faulkner for J. Sainsbury PLC, now out of print); photographs by Vernon Morgan, stylist Maria Jacques, home economist Mandy Wagstaff

56 – 59 Recipe from Chez Solange, 35 Cranbourn St, London WC2

60 – 63 Recipe from 'The French Menu Cookbook' by Richard Olney (a Jill Norman book; Dorling Kindersley, £12.95)

64 – 67 Recipe from 'Caribbean Cooking' by Judy Bastyra (Windward, £7.95)

68 – 71 Recipe by Gilly Cubitt, from Family Circle

72 – 75 Porters English Restaurant is at 17 Henrietta Street, Covent Garden, London WC2

78 – 81 Recipe from 'Cooking with Michael Smith' by Michael Smith (Papermac, £5.95)

82 – 85 Recipe from 'A New Book of Middle Eastern Food' by Claudia Roden (Penguin, £12.95); stylist Carol Pastor

86 – 89 The Wellington Club is at 116 Knightsbridge, London SW1; stylist Carol Pastor

90 – 93 Recipe from 'Mexican Cookery' by Lourdes Nichols (Collins, £9.95); stylist Lorrie Mack

94 – 97 Recipe from 'Perfect Pasta' by Valentina Harris (Granada, £8.95)

98 – 101 Recipe from 'The Sunday Times Complete Cookbook' presented by Arabella Boxer (Weidenfeld and Nicolson, £11.95) Copyright (c) 1983 The Sunday Times

102 – 105 Recipe from 'Middle Eastern Cookery; by Arto der Haroutunian (Century Publishing Company, £9.95)

106 – 109 Recipe from 'The Curry Club Indian Restaurant Cookbook' by Pat Chapman (Piatkus, £7.95); photographs by Vernon Morgan, stylist Maria Jacques, home economist Mandy Wagstaff

110 – 113 Recipe from 'New English Cookery' by Michael Smith (BBC, £5.50); stylist Carol Pastor

114 – 117 Recipe from 'Chinese Cookery' by Ken Hom (BBC Publications, £5.25); stylist Lorrie Mack

118 – 121 Recipe from 'A Taste of Dreams' by Josceline Dimbleby (Sphere Books Ltd, £1.95); stylist Carol Pastor

122 – 125 Recipe from 'European Peasant Cookery: The Rich Tradition' by Elisabeth Luard (Bantam Press, £15)

126 – 129 Recipe from 'The Pizza Express Cookbook' by Peter Boizot (Arrow Books, now out of print)

130 – 133 Recipe from 'A Taste of the West Country' by Theodora Fitzgibbon (Pan Books, £2.95)

136 – 139 Recipe from 'The Observer French Cookery School' by Anne Willan (Macdonald Futura, £9.95); photographs by Laurie Evans

140 – 143 Recipe from 'Katie Stewart's Cookbook' by Katie Stewart (Victor Gollancz, £10.95); photographs by Christine Hanscomb

144 – 147 Recipe from 'The Observer French Cookery School' by Anne Willan (Macdonald, £9.95)

148 – 151 Recipe from 'The Perfect Cook', a selection of recipes by Bernice Hurst (Elvendon Press, £9.95)

152 – 155 Recipe adapted by Raymond Blanc from his original in 'Recipes from Le Manoir aux Quat' Saisons' (Macdonald Orbis, £17.50)

156 – 159 Recipe from 'Cooking for Family and Friends' by Philippa Davenport (Jill Norman and Hobhouse, £8.50); stylist Carol Pastor

160 – 163 The Cordon Bleu Cookery School is at 114 Marylebone Lane, London W1M 5HH,

164 – 167 Recipe from 'Martha Stewart's Pies and Tarts' by Martha Stewart (Sidgwick & Jackson, £13.95)

168 – 171 Turners restaurant is at 87 – 89 Walton Street, London SW3

172 – 175 For more of Mary Norwak's Old English recipes, see the 'Lark Rise Recipe Book' (Century, £9.95)

178 – 181 Recipe from 'The Pastry Book' by Rosemary Wadey (David & Charles, £7.95); stylist Carol Pastor

182 – 185 Recipe from 'The Roux Brothers on Pâtisserie' (Macdonald, £15)

186 – 189 Recipe from 'The Ultimate Chocolate Cookbook' by Jennie Reekie (Ward Lock Ltd, £6.95); photograph on p.186 by Vernon Morgan, stylist Maria Jacques, home economist Ricky Turner

190 – 193 Recipe by Lizzie Boyd

194 – 197 Recipe from 'English Bread and Yeast Cookery' by Elizabeth David (Penguin, £4.95); stylist Carol Pastor

198 – 201 Recipe from 'Bread & Yeast Cookery' by Glynn Christian (Macdonald Guidelines, £2.95), with extracts from 'Glynn Christian's Delicatessen Cookbook (Macdonald, £9.95); stylist Lorrie Mack

202 – 205 Recipe from 'The Country Kitchen' by Jocasta Innes (Frances Lincoln, £9.95)